THE UNITY TAROT

CHOOSE A NUMBER
BETWEEN 1 AND 100
TO FIND SOLUTIONS

Rosie Jackson

THIS BOOK IS DEDICATED
TO ALL READERS

May you be blessed with
intense curiosity,
deep compassion,
the desire to overcome all obstacles,
and the thirst to fully understand

for these will move you forward on your spiritual path,
enabling you to contribute to the
rebuilding of a new world

My deepest gratitude goes to all those
unseen entities who have provided me with inspiration
on this particular creative journey

Endless thanks also to Frederik Basho
for his constant love, encouragement and support
during this project, and for providing the name
THE UNITY TAROT

Rosie Jackson

Bibliografische Information der Deutschen Nationalbibliothek:
Die Deutsche Nationalbibliothek verzeichnet diese Publikation in der
Deutschen Nationalbibliografie; detaillierte bibliografische Daten sind im
Internet über http://dnb.dnb.de abrufbar.
Herstellung und Verlag: BoD – Books on Demand, Norderstedt
Erste Auflage Dezember 2021
ISBN: 978-3-754342565

THE DIVINE PILGRIMAGE

"While the distant goal may seem worthy, it may simply turn out to be a disappointing bauble, shining only because a certain light was shining on it. This "certain light" is your desires, your colouring, propelled by your experiences. Walking towards such "baubles" and the resulting disappointment have one great benefit: they enable you to turn around and reassess your past from a different perspective, and they urge you to take up your divine pilgrimage in a new and more authentic direction, in more alignment with the GOOD OF ALL, as opposed to in alignment with a personally interpreted whim"

From Seraphin Message 217

THE UNITY TAROT

CONTENTS

100 STORIES AND 1000 QUESTIONS

INTRODUCTION

Whenever you find yourself in a difficult situation, this book is one tool which may ease your passage. All problems can be solved through personal work on oneself, as the 100 stories in the Unity Tarot demonstrate, whether these problems are tensions in personal or professional relationships, or whether they are material or financial in nature.

All problems are solved through changes in behaviour and an increase in consciousness. Once all personal issues are solved, community, national and global issues will be solved automatically. Understanding oneself better and improving mental health is also a way of preventing illness. Those who have a very high level of spirituality are more capable of counteracting illness, or it does not even arise. Our collective aim is thus to raise the positive vibrations in ourselves and thus in our world to produce a healthy and harmonious environment.

Sometimes we are so "bogged down" in our own routines, structures and behaviours that it seems impossible to escape this "box". If we manage to step "outside the box", we may see that what we think is true, is actually false, and vice-versa.

How can we do this? One option is answering provocative questions which widen our perspectives and help us to dig deeper. Questions are a great way of promoting discussion, inspiring creativity, encouraging self-reflection and growing our minds.

Another option is contemplating stories featuring protagonists from other countries, and seeking our similarities with them, despite our differences. Stories can take us into another world, can invite us to identify and sympathise, can help us to question our own behaviour without feeling accused. The great soul we know as Jesus was a master of this trade, telling fictive parables to illustrate a point without pinpointing anyone in particular. These

100 stories are designed to assist readers on their spiritual journey, opening up new vistas, opportunities and directions. They provide insights, shake up superstitions, encourage action and flexibility, dissipate stagnation, break the slave mentality, revive creative powers, invite reassessment and foster true values.

HOW TO USE THE STORIES

Close your eyes and imagine you are climbing a steep path up a mountain. The path symbolizes the problem or difficult situation you are presently dealing with. When you reach the top of the mountain, new horizons suddenly open up to you. On the furthest horizon, you will see a very large number between 1 and 100. Then open your eyes and look up the story and positive quality which you will find under that number.

For example, if you saw the number 17 on the horizon, you will find MANIFESTING VISIONS under number 17 in this book, and you will also find the story of a Chinese country girl who suddenly finds herself in the huge city of Beijing, China. Increased manifestation of her vision resolves her problems. You will have chosen 17 yourself intuitively, and so you are now invited to focus on MANIFESTING VISIONS in your own life. If you practice it daily, this will be the solution for you also.

Read the story about the experiences of the Chinese girl slowly, taking it all in. Then answer the questions which follow. If there is a specific question which "jumps out" at you, or which is particularly meaningful for you, this means that it is particularly relevant and that it should be given more attention.

HOW TO USE THE QUESTIONS

Which conviction is so strong and inflexible that it requires a major accident or calamity to wake you up and put you on a different course?

Which part of yourself have you imprisoned, extinguished or kept 'underground'?

What are your 'lost years'?

Supposing you view them as a necessary preamble to a transformation which is on your soul agenda?

What was your last 'wakeup call', and did you take it seriously?

These questions touch on the major issues of our time. They serve to expand our way of thinking and our perspective. This book can be used night and day to solve any issue. If you have not much time for reading stories, then just open the book at random and put your finger on a question. Hold the question in the back of your mind as you go through your daily routine. You can "forget" it, so to speak, until something happens which presents you with a challenge. When you are trying to solve this problem or issue or argument, REMEMBER the question, and this will help with the solving process. Instead, you can of course choose a quality, by selecting a number between 1 and 100, and try to increase your manifestation of this quality during the day.

Why does this work? There is something called DIVINE TIMING. If you carefully examine various encounters and experiences in your past, you will notice many sudden synchronicities, opportunities and inspirational ideas, as well as sudden blockages which prevent disaster. We can call this the workings of DIVINE HAND, construed by benevolent unseen beings, by angels or by sparking ideas presented by YOUR OWN DIVINE INTUITION.

You contain a divine inner spark, as it were, which can be accessed for helpful information, if you ask. Your increased awareness of such signs and impulses, placed in your path at exactly the right time, will reinforce in you the conviction that you are always divinely guided.

It is impossible, therefore, to choose a "wrong number". Participants in my seminars who have rejected their number / quality, wanting to choose another, are rejecting the gift which divine timing is offering them and are actually not sincere or determined enough in their desire to work on themselves. Fear is also a major factor in this. I would suggest that you just experiment, and that this will lead you to trust in the process.

THE HISTORY OF THE UNITY TAROT

Following in the footsteps of the industrial revolution and the technological revolution, there is now necessity for a SPIRITUAL REVOLUTION. Our collective spiritual progress has not kept pace with technological progress, thus new scientific developments are used for war as opposed to creating abundance for all.

What will change when everyone is willing to go through the process of self-development and increasing awareness, when they realise and walk their DIVINE PATH, when they are compassed by compassion, and when they assume full responsibility for themselves and for others?

This Spiritual Revolution – a worldwide rise in consciousness - will end racism, enemy images, environmental harm, human rights abuses, sexual exploitation and the threat of nuclear self-annihilation. If we respond to this "wake up" call, and are continuously aware of our thoughts and actions, we can personally participate in the positive development of world history. Harmony and peace can be attained IF EVERYONE genuinely seeks to discover the conflicts and obstacles in themselves which prevent fruitful relationships and cooperation. Increased critical assessment combined with deep compassion are the qualities which will achieve inner revolution leading to inner peace. In turn, this will LEAD TO OUTER PEACE ON A GLOBAL SCALE.

THE SPIRITUAL REVOLUTION PROJECT

In 2005, the artist Rosie Jackson made a mental note of the fact that different people were always sending her the same text which began "If the world was a village of 100 people", and she decided that this was not coincidence, but divine synchronicity. Using the global statistics in this text (concerning nationality, religion, living conditions etc.) she invented 100 "global villagers" – each of whom represented 1% of the global population - and wrote their biographies. Then she depicted these "global villagers" in a 5-metre-long painting entitled THE WORLD-REALITY, illustrating the whole range of human problems on earth.

But having done this, she felt she could not just leave it at that, so she spent another 2 years considering how each of the 100 global villagers could turn their lives around if they pursued a certain "positive" quality (such as respect, gratitude or compassion). Then she painted the 100 figures anew, depicting their transformation, in another painting entitled THE WORLD-VISION.

The 100 positive qualities act as the catalyst for the SPIRITUAL REVOLUTION which can transform our world into paradise. The 100 biographies all have a "happy end" and include around 10 pertinent questions. This material now forms the UNITY TAROT which is part of my SPIRITUAL REVOLUTION PROJECT. Many blessings on all readers who engage with this material. With love and gratitude, Rosie Jackson

Next page: THE WORLD-REALITY by Rosie Jackson
and the sculpture DuBuDuA by Frederik Basho

PAINTING: THE WORLD-REALITY

My task was complete, or so I thought. As time passed it seemed impossible to just leave it at that. So then I decided to paint the people again after they had solved their problems.

BEFORE AND AFTER: Global Villager 85 from Nigeria who learns to show GENEROSITY

14

**Third and central panel of the painting
THE WORLD-VISION
By Rosie Jackson**

100 QUALITIES: THE KEYS TO TRANSFORMATION

What qualities must we develop to ensure peace and become "one"? The UNITY TAROT offers 100 "positive" qualities which can serve as a point of orientation. The more we voluntarily and conscientiously adhere to them out of love for ourselves and our fellow humans, the faster we will move towards harmonious living. The transformation of the 100 global villagers does not lie in increased material wealth but in increased demonstration of these positive qualities, and we the readers are invited to manifest them also.

IF THE WORLD WAS A VILLAGE

Imagine a tiny village of 100 people where the demographics of the village mirror the demographics of the world's global population. This is what the village would look like:

NATIONALITY AND RELIGION

60 Asians, 12 Europeans
14 Americans (North and South), 13 Africans, 1 Oceanian
34 Christians, 22 Moslems, 15 Hindus, 14 non-religious,
6 Buddhists, 9 other religions

AGE, HEALTH, LIVING CONDITIONS

51 women, 49 men, 50 are under 26
75 live below the poverty line, 50 are undernourished
3 children are deformed
17 have unsafe water
16 women have been sexually abused

WEALTH

18 are overweight, 20 smoke, 10 drink
6 own 59% of the world`s entire wealth

HOUSING AND EDUCATION

80 have inadequate housing
1 is a refugee
21 cannot read
1 has studied at university level
1 woman is a teacher

GLOBAL POPULATION

1 will soon die. 2 will soon be born

MAIN LANGUAGES

14 speak Mandarin
6 speak Hindi
6 speak Spanish
6 speak English
3 speak Bengali
3 speak Portuguese
3 speak Russian
2 speak Japanese
2 speak German

(Original text, State of the Village Report by Donella Meadows,
Sustainability Institute, USA, c. 2005)

GLOBAL VILLAGER 1: CLARITY

Woman aged 24 from Chongqing, China. Non-religious,
lives in poverty and is undernourished, literate,
speaks Mandarin, is sexually abused

A thin woman is brushing her teeth in a women's labour camp.
She shares the toothbrush she is using with twenty-three other
women prisoners. As so often, her mind is crowded with harrow-
ing memories which circle endlessly in a spiral of painful humili-
ation. A sense of dread grips her heart when she remembers the
weekly political meeting of her work unit. She recalls her name
being called out and officials denouncing her as a practitioner of
a forbidden school of Buddhist thought.

She is flooded with memories of utter desolation and helplessness in face of this accusation. Following deportation, she now
finds herself with hundreds of other women in a rehabilitation
camp which is ruled by leering armed guards. She has no religious beliefs and has been wrongly accused. Some of her fellow
inmates are tortured on a regular basis. She herself has been
raped and lives in fear of it happening again.

Astonishingly, the woman is suddenly released from one moment
to the next. When she asks why, the prison warden states that
her arrest was a mistake, a case of mistaken identity. The woman
receives no apology. Now, back home, she is eternally grateful
every time she is allowed to use her own toothbrush, although
she has no running water or private basin. Instead, she spits into
the gutters of Chongqing, her home and one of China's largest
cities. She is not complaining, as she previously did, about the
stench of the open sewers, the polluted air or the dim, damp room
with the tiny barred window where she works for a pittance as a
seamstress. Instead, she feels gratitude for her freedom, for
every mouthful of rice, for the fresh tangy taste of a lemon. She

is thinking about the barred windows and doors which still incarcerate her new friends. Despite their imprisonment, they were always kind and radiated inner strength.

At the end of the day, the seamstress closes her eyes in secret meditation and prayer, trying intuitively to see what steps to take next – steps which become clearer and clearer the more she connects with divine energy. As she progresses along this path, it becomes more and more obvious what is actually unimportant or peripheral. Slowly, she overcomes her fear of the obstacles in her path, recognizing them as agents of 'good', forcing her to reassess where she wants to go. Like her friends, she is able to create an oasis of calm for herself, irrespective of outward circumstances. She experiments regularly, going to places where chaos rules, in order to practise how to remain focused. Eventually she comes to the understanding that it is possible to exist anywhere if one knows how to build an oasis.

Questions

What is not yet clear?
How are you torturing yourself?
How can you improve the next day?
What if you always followed your intuition?
How often do you create an oasis of calm?
Do you take time daily to contemplate your purpose?
Which small daily pleasures can you be thankful for?
How seriously do you see meditation as a means to clarify?
What prevents you from defining your wishes more precisely?
Given that it is possible to view any situation from a different perspective, who have you 'wrongly' accused? Yourself?
What obstacles have restricted your freedom to show you that you have freedom to act?
Have you understood that you must be clear about your starting point if you are to progress in any direction?
Supposing everyone focussed less on the material and more on their relationships to their fellow human beings?

GLOBAL VILLAGER 2: HELPFULNESS

Girl aged 13 from Hebei Province, China.
Christian, literate, speaks Mandarin

A single candle burns in the grey light of early morning. It is five o'clock, and a young girl is already awake, studying English alone by candlelight at a simple wooden bench. She attends a middle school in the depths of the Chinese countryside, but she dreams of escape. Learning English – and later studying abroad – is the vision which drives her on, which helps her bear the overwhelming feeling of loneliness which pervades her daily life.

For her, this is the ticket to freedom, far away from her irritating family and spoilt brother, far away from the suffocating rules of her community and from her life of rural deprivation. There is no water except for a river nearby, and one set of filthy communal toilets. Most of the 600 pupils are boarders and sleep ten to a room, but she sleeps at home because her family lives and works within the school compound. An hour later, when the six o'clock reveille is played over the loudspeakers, she crams her books back into her shabby green army bag, content that she will be well ahead of her classmates in the next lesson.

When she returns home from school one afternoon, she notices that her small brother is hiding under the quilt on his bed. The girl is so used to being ignored by him that she assumes this is just another variation of turning away. But she gradually realizes that he is actually crying – something which has never happened before. Suddenly, the girl's heart softens towards him and she asks him what is troubling him. Slowly, the boy calms down and opens up towards his sister. As a second child under the "one child one family" policy, he has no right to go to school, and now he desperately wants to learn to read. The girl is astonished to hear that he is so unhappy and offers to teach him. Together they sit in the meadow by the river, sometimes learning new Chinese characters, sometimes just watching the fluorescent green insects and butterflies of brilliant blue. As time passes, the girl realises that she herself was the cause of her own loneliness, and that this dissipates when she embraces her family and classmates.

Now she no longer uses her knowledge to show her superiority, but shares it with others. The lessons she gives her brother by the river are followed by play. They throw stones into the water which ripples and glints in the sunlight, and she knows that she too is sending out ripples of positive energy into her surroundings. The girl treasures the clarity and fluidity of water, trying to emanate it in her behaviour, watching it flow effortlessly and unhesitatingly into every hollow. In the midst of nature, she has no long-term plans or distractions: she can just 'be'. And at night she listens to the gentle frog chorus – a sound so familiar, but a sound to which she never paid much attention before. She recognises its beauty and it lulls her into a long, peaceful sleep.

Questions

What if everyone lived in the present?
To what extent is your loneliness self-imposed?
Which misleading ticket to freedom are you pursuing?
Is your focus on the future blinding you to present issues?
What if you were as clear, fluid and unhesitating as water?
What if everyone realized that it is in giving that we receive?
Could you go into the countryside more often to gain solace?
What sort of ripples do you intend to send out into the world?
What if everyone worldwide were prepared to release their ego?
If you achieve this freedom, can you be sure that you will be completely content?
What if everyone honestly addressed their own needs and those of others?
Do the demands of your ego lead you to overlook the needs of your colleagues or family?

GLOBAL VILLAGER 3: SELF EXPRESSION

Boy aged 8 from Hebei Province, China.
Christian, literate, speaks Mandarin

A small Chinese woman stands somewhat helplessly in front of her son. His behaviour is often confusing: he is excited and then subdued, hyperactive then listless, friendly and then suddenly aggressive. Now he refuses to answer any of her questions and she has no idea why he is angry. In the end, she offers him a piece of sugar cane and the boy runs off to a field near the river to eat it in peace. He often plays there by himself, churning up the sandy soil with a stick, and if anyone disturbs him they are lucky not to get hit.

The boy knows that no one can understand how confused he feels. He is made to feel special because he is the son his parents always longed for, but as the second child under the "one child one family" policy, he is also 'illegal' and somehow wrong. Perhaps, if he tries to do enough good deeds during his lifetime, the yellow crane will fly him up to heaven, but he does not know how to start. Perhaps he should try and take a bus to the famous Yellow Crane Pagoda in Wuhan to ask for help? Perhaps the yellow crane will be angry if he does not stop being bad?

The boy also wants to learn to read, but he cannot. He is not allowed to go to school like his elder sister. When she ignores him, he feels upset and runs away whenever she comes home. The next time the boy refuses to answer her questions, his mother suddenly explodes with rage and leaves him alone. The boy runs to his bed, hides under his quilt and starts to cry for the very first time. To his great surprise, his sister comes up to him and speaks to him softly, asking him what the matter is. Gradually, he finds words to express the confusion he feels, and confides his secret desire to read.

When she offers to teach him, he can hardly believe it. Could she really be so very different from what he had always thought? When he worries about the yellow crane, he tells his mother. She cradles him in her arms and says that the yellow crane temple is not something to be afraid of. If a god exists, she thinks that he cannot be angry. Probably he or she is a caring and generous person who doesn't have any rigid or confining rules.

The young boy realizes that the more he expresses his fears and desires, the more content he becomes. The sudden explosions of anger which shocked his playmates are on the decrease. When the boy is happy, his enthusiasm is infectious and he dances around with the other children in the compound. He realises that he is special and that everyone else is special too.

Questions

Are you aware of how special you are?
Do you regard other people as special?
What if the 'divine' or 'god' never punishes?
Suppose it is impossible to make mistakes?
Which feelings have you not fully expressed?
What makes you feel 'wrong'? Are you wrong?
What would you do next if everything was 'allowed'?
In what way could your behaviour be judged as confusing?
Is there anyone you are ignoring or not fully acknowledging?
What fear causes a dreadful feeling whenever you ask for help?
How often does your judgment of what is 'good' or 'bad'
determine your behaviour?
Supposing you voice your emotions the moment you feel them?
What if 'punishment' is a result of negative individual and
collective energy?
How would the world change if our decisions were not based on
what we personally consider 'good' or 'bad', but on what 'works'
for us and what 'works' for the world?

GLOBAL VILLAGER 4: COMMUNICATION

Girl aged 9 from Qinghai, China. Non-religious, lives in poverty and is undernourished, literate, speaks Mandarin

On the banks of a wide river in western China, a huge Buddha has been carved out of a cliff. Sitting on the Buddha's toe, a small girl crouches with her knees pulled up tightly to her chin. She lives with her parents in one dark room with a small window.

In the afternoons, when her schoolwork is done, she is allowed to go out by herself for an hour. Rushing down the crumbling brick stairway, she escapes from the old, musty building into the light and on towards the river where the stone Buddha towers above the water.

She watches boats bringing new tourists. Their clothes and language are strange to her. Their voices seem loud and coarse, and she resents the way they swarm over the Buddha's feet.

When foreign tourists want to take a picture of her sitting on the Buddha's toe, she turns away, indicating that the sun is too strong for her eyes. Scowling, she covers her face with her hands and wishes they would stop interfering and leave her favourite place alone for ever.

One day, the girl takes her usual afternoon walk to the Buddha to find her path blocked by a fence: as an important historical site, it requires some renovation. The child is devastated. It seems that her favourite place is not actually hers at all.

For two long weeks, she is not allowed in. When it is finally reopened, she skips over the Buddha's feet and sings with delight. Visiting Chinese tourists capture her joy on film, and she tells them why she is so happy. In return, they tell her interesting stories about their travels, describing wild birds on a big lake to the west, and telling her about a sprawling Lama monastery an hour away where beams are painted in brilliant colours and where the air is alive with the sound of smiths hammering metal.

The girl listens attentively to these stories. She also attempts to greet foreign visitors with smatterings of English which she has picked up from an old text book. They laugh and sometimes take a picture of her sitting on the Buddha's feet, holding a large leaf over her head for a sunshade. But instead of sitting on the big toe – a favourite place for taking photographs – she leaves it free for others, preferring to sit on the middle toe instead. When one lady asks for her address and promises to send her a postcard, the girl can hardly contain her excitement. Every morning she rushes to the post-box in feverish anticipation.

Questions

Do you notice others?
How do you approach them?
What fear lies behind your reactions?
What role does your ego play in conflict situations?
Does any place or any person belong entirely to you?
What if you share more of your personal experiences?
What if everyone you meet had a personal message for you?
What prevents you from improving your communication skills?

How would the world change if there were no 'foreigners',
only sisters and brothers?

How do you react – or overreact – when others encroach
on your privacy?

How would the world change if all encounters could be
perceived as inspiring and uplifting?

GLOBAL VILLAGER 5: DEEP PERCEPTION

Woman aged 25 from Hunan, China. Non-religious, literate, speaks Mandarin, sexually abused

A pregnant woman is sitting at a simple wooden table opposite her husband. Her defiance of official rules has put her in a dreadful predicament. Her determination to have a child as soon as possible has blinded her to the necessity of applying beforehand for official permission from the family planning bureau.

Every day for the last month, work unit officials have burst into their cramped flat. They have torn the newspaper off the walls, glued on to keep out the damp. They have spat on the concrete floor, used up all the coal and eaten all provisions. Practically nothing is left.

The officials insist that aborting the baby is for the communal good and that everyone must adhere to the "one child one family" policy if the country is to survive. The woman and her husband feel powerless to act and put on a brave face. Finally, the woman admits defeat and goes to the family planning bureau to say that she will undergo an abortion.

Following the operation, the woman gives into her pain. Expression of her torment at losing the child triggers off other memories of unexpressed grief which she has long since buried in the past. She admits to her husband that she was sexually abused in her youth, thus hindering true understanding and communication in their own relationship. In their subsequent long conversations, they learn more deeply about each other's needs and fears.

They are sad that their plans to have a child have been thwarted in a terrible and inhumane manner, but they also recognise that it has actually improved their own personal development as a couple – and will thus benefit any child they have in the future.

They decide to wait a bit longer before starting a family. Much later, they come to the very difficult realisation that the aborted child was an angel who chose them as parents in order to bring them this understanding.

The woman becomes increasingly attuned to her own needs and wishes. She enjoys a new, deep intimacy with her husband and learns to assist others using her increased powers of perception. Later she is able to meet the challenges of raising a child with grace and maturity.

Questions

Are you powerless?
How often do you show your pain?
How often do you put on a 'brave face'?
How much of your life is already planned?
What choices have you had the power to make?
Supposing we are all gods and goddesses with immense power?

How often do you decide to go ahead with fixed plans without communicating them?
What would happen if you looked deeper, beyond the story to the reason for the story?
Are your actions attuned to your real desires?
Given that everyone has 'time', do you use it for what you consider important?
How much time do you consciously set aside for relaxation, meditative rituals or 'nothing'?
What 'dreadful' events have you created to provide yourself with greater insight?
Supposing everyone in the world was fully aware of the fact that every negative action and every negative thought has a negative impact on our environment?

GLOBAL VILLAGER 6: INTEGRITY

Man aged 23 from Inner Mongolia, China.
Non-religious, literate, smokes, speaks Mongolian

A pile of ropes and household utensils lies on the ground, spread out on a worn cloth. A man crouches stiffly beside it, hoping that he will sell enough to buy food for the day. His present daily grind is fairly monotonous, making a meagre living from reselling an assortment of items sold to him by an acquaintance. Whereas he suspects that these may be stolen goods, he asks no questions. Every day is the same, squatting placidly at the edge of the street, without much hope for the future. Although he senses that he could make more of his life, he prefers to keep to familiar places and people.

One morning, the man bumps into his supplier who is carrying a large statue of a dragon. He insists that it will bring a lot of money at the market and, although the seller's first impulse is to refuse, something makes him take the dragon away with him. It triggers memories of a visit to Wudang Monastery as a child. The man relives the sudden sense of wonder he felt when confronted by a huge statue of a dragon in the monastery grounds. As a small boy, he imagined flames shooting out of the dragon's nostrils and turning into a large fire, just as big as the huge uncontrolled coal fires where his father worked in Ningxia Province.

As a small boy, he playfully put his head into the dragon's mouth and laughed. The man is filled with sorrow at his present lack of youthful energy and daring, and he decides to revisit Wudang to regain inspiration. When he finds the dragon again and puts his head into its mouth, he suddenly knows that he has got to change. He decides to confront his supplier about the stolen goods and discovers that his suspicions are well-founded.

Although he feels strangely 'empty' because he has lost his source of income, he realises that everything which is empty is also full of potential and possibility. He starts to regard the world in a more critical way. Buddhism becomes increasingly attractive to him with its emphasis on learning and questioning rather than accepting assertions uncritically. The man is especially attracted to Tibetan Buddhism in which form is emptiness and emptiness is form. Neither is real or unreal. Both are existent and non-existent. Full of optimism and vitality, he turns a new page in his life and is led by the principle of integrity.

Questions

What have you 'stolen'?
Is it time to take a break?
Who do you need to confront?
How can you light your hidden inner fire?
Have you stolen something from yourself?
How much of your behaviour is controlled?
How can you ignite your own divine energy?
Is it time to take concrete steps in a new direction?
What extraordinary act would lift you out of passivity?

Can you imagine that you are holding on to something which prevents you from experiencing abundance?

What if turning a new page in your life reveals an empty space full of potential?

What would happen next if you lost your fear and started to question critically?

What if no-one simply accepted and became critical?

What if the actions of every member of our planet were governed by integrity and honesty?

GLOBAL VILLAGER 7: MINDFULNESS

Woman aged 25 from Xingiang, China. Muslim, lives in poverty and is undernourished, literate, speaks Kazak

It is dawn on the snowline of the Tien Shan Mountains in northern China, and a woman dashes outside to fill her blackened kettle with snow. Her eyes dart fearfully beneath her green headscarf, and her reddened cheeks are roughened by wind. She carries wood, churns milk, cooks, cleans, sews and breastfeeds, giving continuously without a second thought. She tends the children and the goats, but she hardly ever speaks, resenting her isolation on the mountain.

Late that evening the men return on their horses after successfully selling some of their animals. As they sit cross-legged round the fire drinking, they decide kill the last kid to celebrate the occasion. The woman feels a shudder of terror but covers her face to hide her feelings. She lies motionless under the furs next to her small sleeping son, but she knows that the goat's head is being roasted over the fire in the flickering semi-darkness of the yurt.

When the small boy awakes, he runs outside to greet his pet goat, but he cannot find it. When he asks his mother where it is, she breaks down and cries. This sudden, intense and genuine expression of feeling is the first step towards breaking through the overwhelming numbness and resignation which has governed her life so far. Although the woman's role as helper and provider changes very little, she is now more conscious of what she does and how she does it. She completes her chores in her own time, under no pressure, and she no longer emits an air of surly servility.

Instead of rushing outside quickly to fetch snow for the kettle, she wraps herself up warmly and walks slowly, pausing to wonder at the crystallized grass and slender fingers of ice crunching beneath her feet, showing these natural wonders to the child whose hand she holds. Invigorated by the wind, she turns eagerly to search the sky for the first faint orange tinge of light on the mountain ridge which heralds the arrival of the morning sun. She remembers the bus-loads of sightseers, the grazing cattle, the snaking roads and the snarling traffic further down the valley, and she is grateful for this moment of early morning silence which starts her day.

Questions

Are you are continuously giving?
What do you expect as a result?
Can how you recover your vitality?
Are you mindful of every moment?
What avenues are always open to you?
What acute problem is it time to discuss now?
How much responsibility do you take on for yourself?
How much do you take on for the people around you?

Do you consciously invite moments of silence or periods of rest into your life?

How could you welcome each day as if it offers infinite new opportunities?

Are you stubborn or unwilling because you think you have no choice?

How can a change in your consciousness turn unpleasant or unchangeable situations into a new experience?

What if everyone in the world were continually aware of all the choices available to them?

GLOBAL VILLAGER 8: LEADERSHIP

Woman aged 35 from Xingiang, China.
Muslim, literate, speaks Uighur and Mandarin

Grasping her throbbing head in her hands, a cotton worker in western China is haunted by fear and by the unpleasant memories she has bottled up inside her. She is a member of the Uygur minority race, and she works in a large factory. Lethargic, ragged and hungry because she has not been paid for five months, she has to rely on the benevolence of her neighbours who give her their scraps of left-over rice.

She feels deserted, especially by the men in her life; by her father, who worked in southern China and only returned to his family once a year; by her first husband, who never showed his feelings and disappeared without explanation overnight; and by her present husband – a miner – who failed to comfort her when she lost a child. She envisages these three men with indistinguishable features floating impassively above her, out of reach. Even when she is in a relationship, she feels strangely distant and helpless, desperate for the sense of security she has never known.

When the woman learns that her second husband is dead - one of 80 miners killed in a fatal gas explosion due to negligent safety regulations - she is overwhelmed by a feeling of paralysis and grief. Why does the pattern keep repeating itself? In a bid to change this pattern, she examines her feelings more and more. When she digs deep enough, she finds the core of intense anger and frustration which she has bottled up for so long. She finds herself screaming.

With time, she realises that she is partly screaming at herself, as she recognises that she is fifty percent responsible for her failed relationships. And with time, she understands that the people who deserted her were merely mirroring her own self-desertion. After screaming sessions, she feels a sort of prickling energy coursing through her veins, and for the first time in years she stops grumbling and finds the strength to take action.

She talks to other workers at the factory and realises that they have to make a stand instead of adhering to the role of the suffering victim. Together they draw up a manifesto of their demands and threaten to strike if they are not paid. The woman realises that her past experiences – however painful – are all helpful stages of a process intended to propel her along the path to true autonomy, independence and leadership.

Questions

Have you deserted yourself?
In what way can you become a 'leader'?
What message are unfortunate events trying to give you?
What is your own 'sensitive spot' which is easily wounded?
If you wrote a manifesto for yourself, setting out your own
needs, what would you or your body demand?
Could lethargy be the result of spending large amounts of energy
on keeping emotions – especially anger – under control?
Why are some people angry or hurt when they are deserted,
and others not?
How can you release the anger which is still bottled up inside
you without hurting others?
In your relationships with other people, which patterns keep
repeating themselves?
Given that we create our own lives, how much of your life do
you chose to create?
What new horizons will open when you have successfully let
go of the past?
How would the world change if everyone chose positive roles
in the knowledge that they are role models for others?

GLOBAL VILLAGER 9: TRANSPARENCY

Man aged 48 from Tibet, China. Lamaist, literate, imprisoned, speaks Tibetan and Mandarin

The hand of this monk is clutching the bars of his prison window, while the rest of his body shudders with cold. The window frames the blue-grey mountains of the Tibetan plateau. Though the slopes are barren, the monk recalls the green forests of his youth, now ruthlessly felled by the Chinese. Even now he can hear the indistinct roar of trucks in the far distance – the endless convoy of trucks transporting even more felled trees to China. He has heard rumours about the widespread planting of new, genetically manipulated trees, and though they are not here on the slopes opposite his prison window, he thinks they cannot be far away.

Why didn't he take action sooner to prevent the pillage of his country? He quenches a strong urge to shout, protesting China's ruthless exploitation of Tibet's natural resources, aware that this would be deemed 'unpatriotic behaviour' and that it would pro-long his prison sentence. He curses the Chinese for their insen-sitivity, arrogance and nationalism.

During meditation, the monk receives a vision from a deity, Black Tara, the only saint to whom he did not pay due reverence in his monastery because she was a woman. In the vision, Tara re-minds him that the outer world is a mirror of his inner world, and she instructs him to contemplate his own insensitivity and arro-gance. Humbled, the monk considers his elevated position in the monastery and the way he withheld his disapproval of the Chi-nese authorities to keep this position. He thinks about the vivid scarlet robes he used to wear and the playful discourses on phil-osophical subjects in which he boasted a certain prowess. He remembers showing tourists the precious artefacts and intricate gold painting on the red entrance gates, stating with pride that his monastery was the most beautiful and spiritually significant.

With sadness, he recognises the barriers he has set up around himself, his estrangement from the other monks and his loneliness. Even if he were allowed visitors, nobody would come. He remembers the words of the Buddha, "It is your mind which creates this world", and so he uses his time to meditate on changing his attitude. Realising that his physical limitations reflect his locked-up mind, he begins to see things more transparently. He recognises that sending more anger and condemnation into the world means that there is more anger and condemnation in the world, so instead of attacking perpetrators, he seeks to negotiate. He regrets his pride and sees his imprisonment as a self-made mind prison, a painful stepping-stone to higher awareness.

Questions

Which of your 'achievements' estrange you from others?
What if everyone went 'within' in the face of outside chaos?
Is there any way in which you have imprisoned or
compromised yourself?
How comfortable are you with the thought that your
outer surroundings are a reflection of your inner self?
To what degree does your fear of repercussions prevent
you from speaking your mind?
When was your last uncontrollable urge to speak out and
did you follow that urge?
What if nobody bought any more newspapers and
nobody cut any more trees?

Given that your mind creates the world you see,
which world do you choose to create and which
principles determine your path now?

What unpleasant 'rumours' with catastrophic potential do you -
individually, or as part of humanity as a collective –
choose to ignore rather than investigate?

GLOBAL VILLAGER 10: SINCERITY

Boy aged 14 from Shanghai, China. Christian, lives in poverty and is undernourished, illiterate, speaks Mandarin

Like hundreds of other Chinese Catholics on Sunday mornings in southwest Shanghai, this teenager is on his way to Xujiahui Cathedral. His unobtrusive demeanour and polite smile do not betray his inner turmoil, and his worn but clean clothes do not reveal his lack of financial means. In his mind's eye, his arms are outstretched above him, carrying a huge box of sins to church, walking along the path of penitence which leads to absolution and purity.

He pretends to read the hymn book, for he is ashamed of his lack of education and it would be dreadful to admit that he cannot read. His dreams include unlimited access to books and libraries, and of being respected for his knowledge. His feelings of discomfort are somewhat reduced by being able to go to confession, but he still pales when he recalls the lies he has told, the food he has stolen and the insults he has made without thinking. When he comes out of the cathedral he feels a little more purified and, on the homeward journey, he tends to smile at people, rather than gaze at Shanghai's putrid backstreets or sparkling new towers.

One Sunday, the boy is pretending to read the hymn book as usual, when the man next to him whispers that he is holding it upside down. The boy is absolutely appalled that he has lost face, but the man just laughs gently. Flooded with immeasurable relief, the boy begins to pray. Now, in his mind's eye, he has set aside his box of sins. Instead, he carries a huge amethyst, a symbol of sincerity and heavenly understanding, which leads him to a higher spiritual plane. When he goes to confession, he values this as a method to become conscious of fear, which he can then release, but his concept of 'sin' no longer exists. He has learnt that 'losing face' is an opportunity to learn. Instead of cowering with shame, he stretches his arms out to the universe.

With time, the boy turns into a highly respected visionary – a pioneer in thought and action on spiritual and material planes. He can see beyond already existing educational or religious structures while appreciating the core truths of each. Instead of dreaming of a library of books for his personal use, he knows that divine knowledge already exists in every person and in every cell, and that it can be accessed by tapping into universal consciousness. He treats his followers with gentle humour and compassion, encouraging them to live their potential and demonstrate absolute sincerity in their behaviour at all times.

Questions

Can you forgive yourself?
How often do you make excuses?
What role does politeness play in your life?
What fear could you release through 'confession'?
What self-imposed barriers have so far prevented you
from living life fully?
Is it possible to insult someone who is totally centred, confident
of their own worth and governed by love?
Which of your qualities has not been acquired through
conventional education?
Given that we enter life with nothing and leave with nothing
except the insights we have acquired, what is your dream?
How would you act differently if you were convinced that you
have access to divine knowledge?
How would the world change if everyone discovered their
connection to the divine?
What will change when you release your ideas of right and
wrong in favour of what works for you and for humanity
as a collective?

GLOBAL VILLAGER 11: SENSITIVITY

Woman aged 19 from Jingtong, Yunnan, China.
Hinayana Buddhist, literate, speaks Dai and Mandarin

An attractive young woman is being photographed as she peeps coyly into a mirror, regarding her long black pigtail with great satisfaction. At the same time, she remembers the beauty of the dead butterflies which an admirer once showed her at the nearby Botanical Institute. This makes her forget the drearier part of her life - her poorly-paid day job cleaning hostel rooms. During the day, she usually feels as if a dense, grey cloud is hanging continuously over her. She prefers to regard herself as a performer of traditional dance who takes part in late night shows for the Chinese soldiers passing through her small village near the Vietnamese border. During the dance, she deliberately emphasises the sensual movements, provoking titters of laughter from the crowd. At the end, the spectators are so embarrassed that they fail to show their enthusiasm. The girl is offended, and so she is all the more susceptible to the attentions and compliments of a visiting photographer. She is impressed by his huge and hugely expensive camera, and agrees to let him walk her home.

As she unlocks the door and turns to say goodnight, the photographer grabs hold of her and forces his way into her home. Her neighbour comes running when he hears her screams, but the photographer manages to escape. The dishevelled young woman is greatly distressed after this experience and frees herself of all vanity. She realizes that she has been imprisoned by her own self-importance and that she is thus insensitive to others.

Now, when she looks in the mirror, she is no longer checking her appearance. Instead she looks into her own eyes asking "Who am I?" again and again, trying to understand the essence of who she really is. During the day, she goes about her cleaning in a meditative fashion. Occasionally, she stops for a precious moment to watch the black dragon butterflies darting playfully around the giant geraniums. When she dances, she no longer focuses on her sensuality to provoke or embarrass the soldiers. While the sensual element remains, it has become gentle. The hearts of her spectators are touched by the sensitive way she conveys her feelings and compassion, and they applaud her well. Suddenly she realises the significance of the name of her home province of Yunnan, meaning 'south of the clouds'. For her, the clouds have parted and she feels her soul lift with light and love.

Questions

What do you see and feel when you look into a mirror?

What feelings come to the surface when you consider the effortless flight, the natural instincts, the delicate beauty and the brief lives of butterflies? What would you have to change for your life to resemble that of a butterfly?

What small miracle in your immediate surroundings could fill you with inspiration?

What prevents you from seeing yourself and your actions as part of the Divine?

How often do you interpret lack of response from another person as a personal insult?

What role has personal insensitivity or lack of communication played in your life so far?

Which particular 'cloud' or negative issue is receiving too much of your attention?

What would the world be like if everyone danced through life?

GLOBAL VILLAGER 12: JOY IN ABUNDANCE

Man aged 48 from Guelin, China. Taoist, lives in poverty and is undernourished, literate, speaks Cantonese

A farmer is up to his knees in water in a rice field in the mountains of Guelin. As he works, he hears the sound of firecrackers in the distance, part of a funeral ceremony. He already feels old, as if he has not got much more time to live.

As he transplants the new shoots, his movements are mechanical and lethargic, as if he is drained by the heat, and his thoughts are clearly elsewhere. His mind is crowded with memories of last year's failing harvest and the way he attempted to supplement his income by selling bamboo trinkets which he had made in his limited spare time.

He feels that he needs more land, more time, more money, more love, more freedom – in fact, there doesn't seem to be 'enough' of anything. When he crosses the small bridge, he sees that the river is choked with weeds because there is not enough water.

When he travels into town to sell his rice, he sees that there is not enough room for him on the bus, though he tries to push and pull at the shoulders of the men blocking his way, and so he is sometimes forced to ride hanging onto the door. He deeply resents anyone who appears to have a lot of money, convinced that they are immoral, selfish and unhappy.

One day on his way into town, the farmer is particularly dejected and frustrated from his battle to get into the crowded bus with two sacks of rice. As usual, the bus is overloaded, and it crawls its way through the mountains on a seemingly endless journey. As it approaches a railway crossing, the bus falters to a stop and the engine breaks down. The farmer sinks into the depths of despair, as if his life has also come to an end.

At that moment he hears the slow, steady clanking of a passing train. A strong animal smell pervades the air, and when he looks up, he sees the eyes of hundreds of pigs peering out of the carriages through wooden slats.

At this moment, the man is fully aware of all his senses and feels incredibly alive. His sympathy for these captive animals on their way to the slaughterhouse is so great that eating them seems like an act of inacceptable barbarism. A wave of intense gratitude floods over him, and he rejoices in his freedom.

When he crosses the bridge on his return home, he does not see a choked river but recognizes that there has been 'enough' water to feed the verdant grass on the river bed. When he returns to his fields, he no longer sees them as a burden, but blesses them as the source of his sustenance. No longer focusing entirely on his land, for fear it will not provide, he lifts his eyes towards the mountains and thinks of the pilgrims climbing to the holy Taoist Temple.

He decides to become a pilgrim too, and as he climbs he is intensely aware of every step he takes and of every twist in the path. It does not take him as long as he thought. His new outlook on life is reinforced by an inscription at the top. It refers to the Taoist attitude to time, to eternal recurrence every 23,000 years.

From the summit, he gazes over the spectacular mountains which stretch into a blue haze on the horizon. The glinting river winds its way between the mountains like a silver snake.

He is filled with a rush of joy at the beauty of this landscape, and he wonders why it has taken him so long to explore and appreciate something which is actually so near.

Questions

Have you got enough?

What if divine sources always provide?

Are you blocking your own path?

How long do you wait before choosing a different path?

What fear leads you into situations which restrict you?

Which area of your life looks as if it is choked with weeds, or has come to a dead end?

Are you aware that condemning wealth is pushing it further away from yourself?

Which activities do you complete in a mechanical manner?

How much time do you spend watching, listening, exploring joyfully and giving thanks?

What if we grow old because we think that we have to grow old?

What if we grow older quicker because we ingest the information of death via meat?

How would your life change if you knew that death is simply crossing a border into a new realm, and if you knew that 'time' is timeless, that life is eternal?

What would the world be like if everyone realised that it is possible to move towards new experiences instead of resigning themselves to 'fate'?

GLOBAL VILLAGER 13

ENJOYMENT

Global Villager 13 as depicted in the painting

THE WORLD – REALITY

By Rosie Jackson

GLOBAL VILLAGER 13: ENJOYMENT

Woman aged 50 from Shaanxi Province, China
Non-religious, lives in poverty and is undernourished
Literate, speaks Mandarin

The Yellow River twists and turns like a metallic snake towards a hazy horizon of distant hills. When it changes course, the water churns round the bends, turning brown with silt, and continues relentlessly. Along its banks, a woman also moves forward continuously, though she cannot compete with the pace of the flow of water. She shuffles along in baggy trousers and her tattered apron flaps in the wind. Four thick bamboo poles are tied together, resting on her shoulders and on the ground, four or five metres behind her. With her arms stretched out on either side, she bends under a huge crucifix.

Straining and sweating under the weight, she focuses on her feet, oblivious of the bicycles passing her, piled high with gas bottles and sacks of salt. She is resigned to carrying her load and resolves to hold out to the bitter end. She has to transport the poles to the building site downstream. There is no alternative way of making ends meet. As midday approaches, a group of barefooted men running along with wheelbarrows of coal shout at her to get out of the way. She does not hear them. Her feeble, last-minute attempt to swerve makes her fall on her side. The sun beats down intensely, the poles cut into her bleeding shoulders, and she is on the verge of complete collapse.

One of the fishermen, whose nets are suspended between the willow trees, notices her stumble and rushes to her aid. Although her inner pride immediately rebels, she allows herself to be helped and bandaged. A group of ragged, barefoot children gather round her and gape. Usually, she would have pushed them away brusquely, but her ankle is twisted and she cannot move. Instead of dealing out verbal abuse, she speaks softly to them, explaining what has happened. She speaks comforting words to a reticent toddler with tear-stained cheeks who is frightened by the sight of blood.

The woman is invited to stay while she recuperates, and the children delight in showing her the insects and flowers they have found. The fisherman is only too happy to tie the bamboo poles together behind his boat so that they float effortlessly downstream to the building site. He is going that way anyway. The woman learns to listen attentively, accept help graciously and to enjoy precious, joyful moments with her new adopted family. In the course of time, she feels more invigorated than ever before, realizing that her own blinkered vision is the sole source of any obstacles she encounters on life's path.

Questions

What can you be thankful for?

Do you associate pain with failure?

In what way are you about to stumble?

How often do you accept offers of help?

Can you view a flower or an insect as a miracle?

What cross have you resigned yourself to carrying?

Can you cry with the ease and immediacy of a small child?

What if 'stumbling' is not a sign of weakness but an opportunity to assess why you have chosen this difficult path and whether it is appropriate for you to continue?

To what extent does personal pride dictate your behaviour?

What do you continue to do although you know intuitively that it is detrimental to your health?

Supposing that obstacles help us to travel faster towards our goal? (as proven in experiments involving obstacles and lasers) Can you see problems in the same light?

What if everyone worldwide discarded their fear of 'losing face' and welcomed 'failure' as an opportunity to learn, instead of developing strategies of self-protection and defence?

GLOBAL VILLAGER 14: HONESTY

Man aged 45 from Shenzhen, China. Non-religious, rich, literate, overweight, smokes, drinks, speaks Cantonese

A sturdy man poses happily in front of his new car against a background of skyscrapers as a colleague takes a photograph. As a businessman in Shenzhen, China's booming enclave near Hong Kong, he can still afford the best of city life, although he is secretly uneasy about the future of his firm. As he smiles for the photo, he is actually thinking of where to lunch. Probably he will go to the White Swan Hotel with its landscaped water gardens – a pristine paradise compared to the crumbling colonial mansions nearby which provide a cramped, warren-like abode for scores of families. But this does not concern the business man: he can already visualise the plump fish he will select from the tank and how delicious it will taste when it arrives freshly fried on his plate. Whether or not the fish will cause his usual indigestion is something he would rather not think about now. After all, he has a variety of pills which will deal with it, if it arises, just as he has a variety of strategies to deal with his employees if they act out of line, start to make demands or become too much of a threat.

When the businessman sees the photo of himself posing in front of his car, he is well satisfied. The car looks sleek and shiny, and he himself looks confident and well-heeled. He is just about to release it for promotion purposes when he notices that there is an elongated dark patch under the car. When he blows the photograph up to see exactly what this is, he is appalled to see that an emaciated beggar was sleeping under his car. Suddenly, he feels as if his life is a worthless lie, as if he is a performer on an imaginary stage which has nothing to do with reality. He is deceiving the world, and he also asks himself how the world might be deceiving him. He wonders how many other things are going on, of which he is unaware.

Immediately, he summons his employees and calls a meeting, admitting that the financial side of the business is starting to flounder. Instead of the usual denial, cutting off their questions with glib, misleading statements, he acknowledges their fears and answers them openly and directly. With an increasing focus upon integrity and absolute honesty, he realises that he still has outstanding debts to pay and apologies to make to partners in previous joint business ventures. Following a period of adjustment, the firm starts to prosper again. The more he 'digests' feelings, sensations and situations fully, instead of denying them, the more efficiently his digestive system works, and his outward reality starts to reflect this increasing flow of energy. He develops a positive mission statement for his firm, based on absolute honesty and transparency, for the benefit of all.

Questions

How afraid are you of competition?
What do you deliberately overlook?
How does this fear make your behaviour less authentic?
What strategies have you developed which prevent intimacy?
What would change if you addressed the roots of a problem instead of its symptoms?
How comfortable are you with the thought that you are responsible for your own physical discomfort?
Which issues in your life still need 'closure', so that they no longer block your vision for the future?
What if we all understood that the help we give and the aggressive competitiveness we send out into the universe returns to us like a boomerang?
What sort of energy would you send out into the world if you believed that the energy and integrity you send out into the world returns to you personally?
What if everyone worldwide realised that "closure" inevitably brings about a new beginning?
What if everyone worldwide were honest all the time?

GLOBAL VILLAGER 15: OPENNESS

Woman aged 66 from Wuhan, Henan, China. Muslim, lives in poverty, is undernourished, literate, beaten, speaks Mandarin

An elderly woman wearing thick-rimmed glasses sits grumpily on a small bamboo stool, constantly muttering complaints and squinting at the shoe insoles she is stitching to sell at the market. She belongs to the Muslim Hui Minority and shows fierce loyalty to her tribe, especially now that the antagonism between Catholics and Hui Muslims in her area has recently exploded into open conflict. She turns her back on her Catholic neighbours and criticises all Muslims who are less devout than herself, especially the younger generation. This is exemplified by her selfish, worldly son who is intent on pursuing his own interests and who rejects his mother's concern. Jealous of the attention poured upon her 'spoilt' granddaughter, and outraged by her son's apparent insensitivity to her needs and values, the woman turns to her religion for solace. She dreams about being saved from poverty and depression by a prophet or saviour, instead of being dependent on her son who finds occasional work as a driver.

One morning she hears shouts, and her son arrives in a state of extreme agitation. He has run over a Catholic girl who is severely injured, sparking off violent riots across the city. The woman is devastated, remembering the loss of her own daughter in a road accident. Now, her son has caused similar grief. He does not yet know how, but he tells his mother that from this time onwards, he will dedicate himself to reconciliation between the Muslims and Catholics.

When the woman sees his great remorse and capacity to empathise, she realises that she has been focusing purely on a few of what she saw as his "insensitive" moments, thus failing register the wealth of positive aspects in his behaviour. She also sees that she reacted strongly to this particular trait because it was familiar to her. Thus, she comes to reflect upon her own insensitivity and selfishness towards others and towards herself. She is now open to everything and everyone. Her greatest joy now is caring for her exuberant granddaughter – a small chubby toddler resembling a ball of purple wool when she wears the jumper her grandmother has knitted for her. Her renewed energy and regained independence of spirit enable her to help her neighbours and the family of the injured girl and, with time, her world expands as she never thought possible. Instead of hoping for a saviour, she turns into a saviour herself.

Questions

Can you let go of your need to be right?
Which part of yourself have you injured or killed?
What prevents your loyalties extending to the whole of humanity?
Is the selfishness you see in others also to be found in yourself?
What unfortunate event is trying to open you up to reconciliation?

How difficult is it for you to accept that the negative qualities in another person are a mirror of yourself?

If your focus changes, is it possible that everything you think is true is only a partial truth?

What if we all learned to love better by starting with friends that we hate?

Is it clear to you that personal or private conflicts are the seeds of global wars?

Given that we are all saviours, what new behaviour will you adopt?

GLOBAL VILLAGER 16: TRUST

Man aged 24 from Guangzhou, Guangdong Province, China.
Adheres to animism – a Chinese traditional belief
Lives in poverty and is undernourished, illiterate
Has unsafe drinking water, speaks Yao and Cantonese

Hundreds of people are lying asleep on the floor of Guangzhou railway station. Like 150 million other migrant workers in China, one of them, a thin mechanic in old overalls, has left his work unit in search of casual labour in the city because he cannot adequately support his family. As he sleeps, he has nightmares about the sufferings of his bedridden wife and small son, about sudden attacks by Guangzhou biker gangs, and about losing his sight. Leaving the countryside was one of a limited number alternatives open to him, including selling blood or donating an eye for money to a hospital specialising in organ transplants. In the end though, he decided to leave for Guangzhou where he survives on one scant meal a day. The rest of the money he saves. He feels intensely insecure, always hopping from one job to another, always worrying that it will be the last. Usually he ends up working on building sites under dangerous conditions. He views everyone he meets with instant suspicion, and each encounter is fraught with the fear of manipulation and fear of extra responsibilities which he feels unable to shoulder.

One day his fears come true. Work is nowhere to be found and he sits dejectedly on the curb watching the traffic pass. Suddenly he feels a strange pressure on his shoulder, as if someone has placed a comforting hand there, but he can see no one. The feeling descends down his arm and goes into his hand. It is as if someone is trying to pull him up into a standing position. The man's first reaction is fear and a determination to resist, but in this – his moment of greatest despair – he moves towards trust and lets himself be led. And so he finds himself walking dreamlike along the streets of Guangzhou, guided by an invisible force which he imagines to be to a huge purple angel. Suddenly, the bikers he usually fears drive past on a flotilla of loud motorbikes and stop right in front of him. They seem to be enjoying themselves. The invisible being releases the man's hand, and he starts to wave and cheer enthusiastically. It seems that one biker is having trouble with his motorbike, and the mechanic immediately offers to help.

Through chance encounters of this nature, in which the man's spontaneous nature and kindness are immediately apparent, he is continually entrusted with small jobs which bring him financial gain and ever-increasing confidence that he will be provided for in the future. Whenever the opportunity arises, he tries to convey the existence of other worlds, telling the story of the purple angel.

Questions

Do you manipulate situations or other people?
What if fear always attracts the thing we are afraid of?
What if despair is looking deeply into self-created darkness?
What if you made your life richer through daily acts of kindness?

If you are in a difficult situation, are you always aware of all the possibilities open to you?
How does your fear of extra responsibility or manipulation affect your encounters with others?
What would happen if you lost all fear and gained an indestructible belief in divine guidance?
What miracle or unexpected event in your life could you ascribe to an angel or divine being?
How would your life change if you knew that you are the sole creator of your 'chances' and 'chance' happenings?
What if everyone throughout the world conducted their lives trustingly and in full knowledge of the fact that everyone else can be trusted?

GLOBAL VILLAGER 17:
MANIFESTING VISIONS

Girl aged 12 from Beijing, China. Adheres to Chinese traditional belief - Confucian, literate, speaks Mandarin

An old postcard is lying face down on the street, and a girl reaches down to pick it up. When she turns it over, she sees a photograph of a ship floating on a lake in the garden of Beijing's Summer Palace. The postcard gives the impression that floating is easy, but for the girl, this word has different connotations. She is a 'floating' child with no proper residence permit and no access to official schools, so she feels like a foreigner and is secretly angry with her parents for moving. Torn between two worlds, living in a limbo, she cannot find her own feet or live her dreams.

Her old world is the world of her poverty-stricken childhood, spent in a small village on the southwestern edge of the Gobi Desert, next to a remnant of the Great Wall of China. She remembers the wall stretching for miles into the hazy distance. As a small child, she spent hours wondering where it went to and what was on the other side. Once curiosity led her to climb the wall, but she slipped on the ice. Her fear of high walls and failed voyages of discovery remain with her to this day. Her mind is clogged by a huge bundle of negative thoughts which have little to do with her present reality in her new world, Beijing. The girl and her parents have moved to China's capital city in search of a better life.

The postcard becomes one of the child's few personal possessions which she keeps in an old tin box. Every so often, she takes it out and looks at it, wondering whether she might ever be able to enter that beautiful garden. She loses interest in everything else and becomes so inactive and quiet that her parents worry about her health and sanity. When they ask her what the matter is, she replies that she must visit the Summer Palace. Her persistence is so great that her mother saves every penny to make this possible. Clutching the postcard of the ship, the girl walks slowly towards the real ship on the lake. To her great astonishment, she realizes that it is made of marble and not floating at all. How can something which looks so light actually be so heavy? She breaks into laughter and starts to run along the lakeside, throwing her old fears to the wind, searching every corner of the park for new delights. Full of new hope, reaching for nothing less than the stars, the girl goes on to follow her dreams and manifest her visions in a world where everything is possible.

Questions

Are you free to act?
What are you secretly angry about?
How are you torn between two worlds?
Which wall would you like to see behind?
Do you need official approval to feel valued?
How could you regard your roots as a positive force?
How can you enjoy life's voyage of discovery better?
How earnestly are you committed to achieving change?
Given that everything is possible, what 'impossible' dream will you realise?
How determined are you and what risks are you prepared to take to realise your goal?
Do you understand the symbolism of the objects and situations you experience?
How do old thought structures affect your view of what you are looking at now?
How far are you prepared to focus on new opportunities instead of thinking "Giving up a part of myself means destroying a part of myself"?
To what extent do you feel 'illegal', and to what extent is this your own interpretation?
What if everyone worldwide reached for the stars and implemented their visions?

GLOBAL VILLAGER 18: FORGIVENESS

Man aged 56 from Wuhan, Henan, China. Christian, literate, speaks Mandarin

A man sitting next to a coal-fired stove cradles his head in his hands. On a small wooden table nearby lies an English-Chinese Bible with a worn, black cover. He remembers the underground church meeting where he prayed for a Christian Chinese constitution, and he remembers the years he spent in a labour camp atoning for this, his 'mind problem'. When he thinks about those lost years, he seethes with internal anger, but it never erupts, boiling incessantly below the surface.

Suddenly someone hammers on the door which he has locked deliberately, and he hears his sister sobbing at the other side. She tells him that her daughter has been run over and injured by a Hui Muslim driver. The man immediately jumps up to let her in and, as he listens, his anger burns stronger and stronger until it finally explodes. He runs through the streets in the Muslim quarter, screaming and inciting revenge. Others join him and a wave of religious and ethnic riots escalate in the huge sprawling grey city of Wuhan.

As the man wanders back home half deranged though the back alleys of Wuhan, he sees an elderly woman standing in a doorway. She is crying so bitterly that he stops, confused. His Christian heart tells him that he should feel compassion, but she is obviously a Muslim woman. Finally, after a moment which seems like eternity, his heart prevails and he decides to ask if he can help. She is grateful for his concerned enquiry and tells him about her son who has injured a Catholic girl. She implores him to help her find the girl's parents so that she can explain that it was not a deliberate act of racism, but an accident. The man is astonished and takes the woman into his arms to comfort her. He knows exactly where to take her – to his sister – and in a sudden flash of deep understanding, he recognizes that nothing in his life has ever happened by chance.

This incredible incident leads him to a completely new understanding of everything he has ever experienced. His exclusion of others had led to his own exclusion in prison. The religious riots presently surrounding him are a reflection of his own religious intolerance. Through this new contact with several Muslim families, he comes to see that his hatred was an illusion based on ignorance. He sees his niece's serious injury as the last and most painful 'wake-up call' in a long series of 'wake-up calls' which he has failed to take seriously. Now he greets everyone with a forgiving and loving heart, especially those who hurt him most, as he recognizes that they were the pivotal force behind his joyful transformation.

Questions

When did you last express your anger?
Which painful loss do you focus on, thus attracting negativity?
Which part of yourself have you imprisoned, extinguished or kept 'underground'?
Given that hatred is based on ignorance, what prevents you from forgiving?
What are your 'lost years', and suppose you view them as a necessary stage to a transformation on your soul agenda?
Which conviction is so inflexible that it requires a major accident or calamity to wake you up and put you on a different course?
What was your last 'wakeup call', and did you take it seriously?
Are you aware that pain is a precursor of potential joyful transformation in yourself?
What would change if all religions were seen as partially valid?
Supposing everyone realised that in pardoning, we are pardoned, and that in pardoning ourselves,
we can enter a new period of vitality?

GLOBAL VILLAGER 19:
THIRST FOR KNOWLEDGE

Boy aged 8 from Yunnan Province, China. Non-religious, illiterate, lives in poverty and is undernourished, speaks Dai

The thud of heavy footsteps startles the young Chinese boy who is hiding in the family's vegetable plot. His father is approaching on the mountain path which leads down to Tiger Leaping Gorge. As usual, his father is sullen and angry. He screams at the boy that it is dangerous to go too close to the edge of the gorge, although the boy is nowhere near. The boy feels that something is dreadfully wrong but does not know what. Everyone in the village seems distracted or sad, as if living under an indefinable threat. Many are on the move, packing their meagre belongings and setting off to some unknown destination. Others turn away in fear when soldiers march through the village putting up official notices. Convinced that his questions would burden the villagers and his family even more, the boy pretends that nothing is wrong and runs to find his mother who works in a small restaurant. Here he sits on top of a pile of cabbages, lulled into security by the familiar sound of clanking metal bowls and hissing woks.

The next time that soldiers appear unannounced in the village, they stick up a poster showing the soles of a pair of shoes, and this causes great consternation. The boy's confusion grows until he can bear it no more, and so he asks the soldiers whose shoes they are. The answer is that they belong to Chen Li Li. The next time his father discovers him hiding in the family plot, he dares to ask why Chen Li Li's shoes are so important. Although he half expects his father to be upset and give some curt, gruff reply, he does quite the opposite. He sits down and tells his son what is happening.

It is much worse than the young boy could have ever imagined. Everyone has to leave Tiger Leaping Gorge because a hydroelectric dam is to be built and the village is to be flooded. The farmers are angry because they have no new fields to go to. The villagers are very frightened because they think Chen Li Li was pushed into the gorge deliberately for protesting against the flooding. They do not believe he slipped by accident because his boots had no profile, as the police would like them to believe. While all this is disturbing news, the boy is relieved to know that there is a concrete reason for the dreadful feeling inside him and that it is not just a figment of his imagination. As he grows older, he manages to remain centred in the midst of chaos and to rely on his intuition to see clearly. His investigative mind enables him to become increasingly conscious of the fact that there is often something completely different going on beneath the surface.

Questions

Which question are you afraid to ask?
Do you pretend that nothing is wrong?
What have you decided not to talk about?
How can problems assist you on your path?
How could you react differently to unpleasant situations?
What are you hiding from and which mystery needs solving?
What if your greatest challenge is how to deal with problems?
Do other people have a distorted view of you because you do not show much of yourself?
Which issue would lose its poignancy if viewed from a different perspective?
Given that your soul has its own divine agenda,
how can anything that happens to you be an accident?
Could your fears be dissipated by finding out more information and concentrating on the present?
What if everyone worldwide questioned suspicious or dubious circumstances the moment they arise?

GLOBAL VILLAGER 20: CARING CONCERN

Woman aged 20 from Taipei, Taiwan. Daoist, literate,
speaks Mandarin, sexually abused

As she wanders through at busy shopping street in Taipei on a
sweltering afternoon, a young woman holds an umbrella in the
hope that this will prevent the intense Asian sun from deepening
her complexion. The dark rings under her eyes are the result of
long working hours, followed by long nights out. As usual, she
stops outside the window of her favourite shop which sells the
culmination of her dreams – a white wedding dress with a golden
handbag. In fact, she stops very briefly at most shop windows,
not to survey their goods but to check her appearance which is
generally her main focus of attention. Her major aim is to earn
enough money for some spectacular new clothes to wear on National Day, a major celebration in Taipei. She also wants to buy
the best and most expensive cream available on the booming
skin-whitening cosmetics market, which produces over 50 new
products a year. She is familiar with most of them. Rumours that
such creams may cause rash or contain dangerous ingredients
are something she ignores, preferring to rejoice in the fact that
they make her look healthier and more educated. This fashiona-
ble young woman would love to talk about all this to her colleagues at the store she works in, but they seem very unfriendly.
However, she is confident that her attractive appearance will always win new friends.

When a new skin product arrives at the store, the young woman
is so excited that she runs off to find her colleagues. She finds
them all, without exception, in the staff room singing Happy Birthday round a huge cake, and she retreats, knowing that she has
not been invited to take part. Seeing her dejected, an elderly colleague talks to her gently, explaining that it is often difficult to get
through to her: she doesn't listen properly to what they tell her,
she says she will do something and then she forgets. She agrees

to do something and then she backs out. This results in a lot of frustration. The others think she is unreliable and uncaring. The young girl, so convinced of her sunny disposition and attractive personality, receives a serious shock and is forced to the sad realization that she actually feels very lonely.

After her talk to the elderly colleague, who advises her lovingly, she understands the connection between her loneliness and her lack of caring concern for others. The more she looks, the more opportunities she sees to assist others, whether at work with her colleagues, or in the streets. Now she rushes to fetch a chair for someone who feels ill, or runs to put her umbrella over a child who is caught in the rain. The more keenly she listens, the more she hears. She closes her eyes at periodic intervals during the day to develop her awareness. With time, her sensitivity becomes so acute that she enters a new realm of consciousness and compassion which benefits herself and all around her.

Questions

Are you listening enough?
Are you burning the candle at both ends?
What stops your divine ability to shine and to attract love?
Do you have a quick turnover of friends, partners or jobs?
Is there discrepancy between what you say and what you do?
To what degree do you judge others according to outward appearances or education?
How often do you rely on things, people or products to bring about changes in your life?
What would you do next if personal inner changes brought more positive and effective change?
What activity do you continue to indulge in although you know that it is detrimental to your health?
What if everyone in the world showed caring concern for their fellow humans at every opportunity?

GLOBAL VILLAGER 21: INNER BALANCE

Boy aged 10 from Tamil Nadu, India. Hindu, illiterate, lives in poverty, undernourished, has unsafe drinking water, speaks Tamil

Clouds of dust fly into the air as a small, thin boy plays with a discarded rubber tyre. Behind him is a huge tree where the villagers like to gather and talk before they go to the temple. Sometimes his mother earns a meagre amount of money selling fish, but for the most part the boy lives on the edge of society, eating very little. Despite this, he looks surprisingly healthy – a handsome, cocky face surrounded by a tangle of greasy dreadlocks on top of a wiry, agile body.

When he plays near the tree, the villagers pay him scant attention. Stealing up to them quietly, he suddenly screams and turns fast cartwheels. In the end, an old wizened man asks him kindly to stop disturbing the peace. Secretly, the boy wishes he could listen to their discussions and go to the temple too. Perhaps he can pray to the deities anyway and strike a bargain with them to get what he wants. But he knows this is impossible because of his dirty clothes and bare feet. Turning away in shame, he scuffles through the streets, convinced of his own insignificance.

The next time the boy approaches the tree, he decides on a different strategy. Instead of causing a disturbance, he sneaks up quietly, sits down and says nothing. The wizened old man notices him out of the corner of his eye, but continues talking to his group of the assembled followers, modulating his language so that the boy can understand easily. The old man continues his story about Gandhi, the man who came from very humble origins but who radiated peace. He invites all his listeners to join him on an outing to the Gandhi Memorial Temple further along the coast. The boy's eyes are shining. Is it possible to achieve fame and respect, despite being poor? Are there other worlds to discover?

Suddenly he decides that his ragged clothes do not matter, and he enters the temple anyway. His senses are intensely aware of the sounds and smells of his surroundings, and a feeling of peace spreads through his restless body. People in white approach him and take his hand, surrounding him in a circle of light. When the boy leaves the temple, he feels as if he is floating. He sits under the village tree and looks upwards, seeing the majestic branches and the birds for the first time, and he is filled with trust as he contemplates the thousands of new leaves which are born again each spring. He rejoices in the endless energy of the sea, and collects shells which he brings to his mother. She, in turn, initiates a cooperative with other women, selling sea products to tourists, and they have a secure income at last. Like the Taoists, the boy grows up with the aim of developing inner balance. As he turns into a man, his greatest wish is to assist others on their path to inner peace and thus to outer peace.

Questions
How resigned are you?
Do you feel under pressure?
How much of it is self-made?
When do you curb your own vitality?
Could you decide on a different approach?
How convinced are you that nature will provide?
How often do you judge from outward appearances?
How will cooperation with others improve your situation?

What strategies do you use or what bargains do you strike in an attempt to gain what you want?
What would you like to do although you do not fit the social requirements?

What will change if everyone was continually inspired by nature's cycle of renewal?
What if everyone put their full trust in the Divine?
How will the world benefit if everyone displayed inner balance?

GLOBAL VILLAGER 22: GENTLENESS

Boy aged 7 from West Bengal, India. Hindu, illiterate, lives in poverty and is undernourished, speaks Bengali

The dark, fearful eyes of a small boy search the horizon for signs of movement. He lives in an isolated village which is rarely visited by outsiders. For the most part, the boy plays with sticks, stones and mud while his mother is out in the fields. His father is in a distant city – no-one quite knows where.

Every day, the boy looks out longingly for the return of his mother and for the return of the neighbour's donkey staggering under its daily load. Three local boys unload it. Then two of them sit on the donkey's back while a third whips it with a stick until it bursts into a trot. The small boy would like to ride too, but he just watches on in silence, his heart pounding with longing. He wishes he were older and stronger.

One day, he summons up all his courage and asks if he can ride on the donkey too. The boys are rough with him and laugh, but a villager intervenes and the child is allowed to ride. With a feeling of great happiness, the small boy climbs onto the donkey's back, but a moment later he is crying. The donkey is so thin that its ribs stick out, and patches of skin show where the fur has been rubbed away.

After only a few steps the boy jumps off again and begins to talk softly to the donkey, stroking it gently, thanking it for the ride, saying he is sorry he hasn't got anything for it to eat.

At first the older boys laugh, but in the end, they are touched by the boy's innocence. Shamed by his gentleness towards the donkey, they begin to treat it less harshly. The small boy's eyes are no longer fearful, but always shining. Love is a quality that he learns to express more and more clearly. When his mother returns from the fields, he runs up to her immediately and tells her how much he has missed her. He also asks incessantly where his father is, instead of pretending he doesn't want to know.

As he grows up, the boy's dedication to animals attracts others who think alike. Together they eventually find a place where the donkey – and other mistreated animals – can recover from past abuse and enjoy their lives to the full. As a man, his zeal leads him to learn to read and to write passionate letters to people in positions of power, drawing their attention to the need for humanitarian treatment of animals.

Questions

Who do you let intimidate you?
How long do you wait until you speak?
What feelings are you not communicating?
Are you aware of the power of your gentleness?
What burden are you carrying?
Whose burden are you carrying?
How much longer do you intend to carry it?
Which burning question would you actually like to ask?

How deeply can you identify with the sufferings of living beings, whether animals or humans?

What strategies have you developed to deal with feeling estranged?

In view of the law of attraction, what sort of energy do you wish to send out and what sort of energy do you wish to attract?

What if everyone worldwide approached all living creatures with gentleness?

GLOBAL VILLAGER 23: IMMEDIATE ACTION

Man aged 25 from Gujarat, India. Hindu, literate, lives in poverty is undernourished, has unsafe drinking water, speaks Gujarati

The sudden sound of shots nearby makes a man stop rigidly in his tracks. This is the last thing he expects to hear in a holy place. The Hindu temple in Gandhinagar, where he wanted to pray, is surrounded by military controls, warning locals to go no further. To his horror, the man realizes that the temple is under siege. Inwardly he recoils when confronted with this eruption of religious violence, especially when he sees that the soldiers are firing indiscriminately through the gates, but he also feels strangely apart. A wounded Muslim struggles towards him and clearly needs help, but the man merely watches. As usual, he is immune to his surroundings and his hands hang limply by his side, inactive and useless. The expression on his face is numb. He has nearly always felt isolated from his fellow humans, especially as a member of the lower caste. As he stands there, two other men jump forward to help the injured man. Paralysed despite the bloodshed happening right before his very eyes, the man vaguely wonders why his desire to assist is not stronger. The whole incident leaves him with a faint feeling of helplessness, but he puts it behind him – as he puts so many unpleasant episodes behind him – as if he has been watching a rather unpleasant film.

A day later the man walks past a tea stall where someone has left a newspaper on a table. He sees an article which covers the conflict at the temple and he is astonished to see a photograph of himself with a vacant expression on his face, while a man bleeds on the ground in front of him. It seems to the man that his barbarity has been officially recorded and put on public display. Feelings of shame and sadness rise from deep within him and he screams out his despair with an immediacy and intensity that he has never before experienced. Several people rush up to him offering help, making him feel even worse.

He resolves to undergo a radical change in his behaviour. Instead of covering up his feelings, he tries to get them out into the open. Instead of looking for help from elsewhere, he now offers it instead, irrespective of the religion, sex or social status of the person concerned. The more he crosses these barriers, the less isolated he feels. The man learns to interpret happenings on a symbolic level and understands that outer conflicts are a mirror of inner turmoil.

In an effort to go into action and see justice done, he talks to many of his caste in Gujarat's coastal areas which were hit by a huge tidal wave, collecting information, documenting their losses and fighting for their compensation. Relief, it seems, has been unfairly distributed. It is a joy to feel active and appreciated, and he is no longer destitute because he is offered shelter and food in return for his help. Leaving passivity behind him, he reacts immediately in every emergency. As he increasingly learns to trust his 'gut reaction', he notices that he 'knows' what is going to happen in advance. With time, this ability of clairgnosis is so developed that he is highly sought after by people in need.

Questions

How quickly do you go into action in an emergency?
Which of your qualities can help and inspire others?
What if you interpreted your surroundings symbolically?
What aspect of your behaviour isolates you from others?
What is your unresolved inner conflict or unhealed wound?
Which sad or unpleasant event do you still have to address?
Which areas of your life require more determined action?
Is the global population immune to the cries of an injured planet?
What if we are intimately connected with all things and if the declining immune system of a damaged planet is mirrored by our own failing immune systems?
What would change if everyone reacted immediately in situations of emergency?

GLOBAL VILLAGER 24: CONNECTEDNESS

Boy aged 8 from Nalgonda, Andhra Pradesh, India, Hindu, lives in poverty and is undernourished, illiterate, has unsafe drinking water, speaks Telegu

With skill and patience, a small boy carries a heavy water pitcher on his head. He brings it to his mother who mixes it with another liquid and pours it on the rice fields. As an 8-year old, he does not really understand that this is pesticide – he is just warned that it is dangerous to drink. But it is not clear to him why it could be good for the rice, or for the people who eat the rice. The confusing thing is that everyone complains that the drinking water is polluted, but they drink it anyway.

The boy has an enquiring mind, but it is not encouraged. The boy would like to go to school, but his mother is pregnant and too ill to earn extra money. The boy himself has bad teeth and a crooked foot, like many others in the village, and everyone knows that these incurable debilitations are caused by the high fluoride content of the drinking water.

Sometimes reporters or government officials appear suddenly in the dust-filled village. They ask questions, assure that they will do their best to change this appalling situation and set a date for piping uncontaminated water to the village. But when the day comes, nothing happens.

The affected villagers feel helpless, and the unaffected villages are largely impervious to the plight of their neighbours and do not feel the need to contribute to other communities outside their own.

When his mother gives birth to a small baby with a deformed body, the boy is shocked and upset. The next time a government official passes through the village, the boy pulls him into the family hut to see the child. The official is so moved at the boy's concern and so distraught by the sight of the baby that he tells everyone in the neighbouring villages and tries to push ahead with the building of the water pipeline.

Meanwhile, the boy understands that his spontaneous action has had a widespread effect. The tired, defeated villagers are astonished that a boy so young should speak so clearly and have such definite ideas. He no longer compromises if he thinks something could be harmful.

As he grows up, he asks precise questions and expects answers. If he loses friends along the way, this does not make him change course. He takes on responsibility for himself and his family.

Later this extends to larger communities – his village and his country. In view of widespread contamination and pollution, it is no longer possible for individuals or nations to ignore each other or to harm the environment in any way.

Sharing inspirational ideas and resources is commonplace, and there is no delay between feeling or seeing distress and taking action to address and eradicate the root cause.

Providing immediate assistance goes unquestioned, as helping others is seen in a broader sense as helping oneself. The boy turns into an inspirational speaker who spreads the message that no one is 'separate' or unconnected.

As a man, he urges everyone to act as responsible members of the Global Family, treating their home and their planet, with the utmost respect.

Questions

Are you in some way 'poisoning' something in your life
or environment?

What drastic measures are you implementing to control
a situation?

If irresponsible behaviour angers you, how is this a mirror of
irresponsible behaviour in yourself?

What if your focus shifted from a personal to a global
perspective?

Do your goals have priority over who is going to accompany
you on your journey?

Given that we are all connected, how do you intend to respond
to the plight of others?

How clearly do you express your opinions?

How long does it take for you to translate your emotions
into action?

How is it possible to bring your deeply felt concerns into
the open?

Which 'root causes' could you address, rather than treating the
symptoms?

How would the world change if everyone saw themselves as
intrinsically linked to one another?

GLOBAL VILLAGER 25
RECONCILIATION

Global Villager 25 as depicted in the painting
THE WORLD – REALITY
By Rosie Jackson

GLOBAL VILLAGER 25: RECONCILIATION

Man aged 69 from Bombay, India. Hindu, literate, has diabetes, smokes, speaks Hindi

There is hardly anyone sitting in the dark lounge of a rather exclusive club dating from British colonial days. Only one guest, an elderly Indian gentleman, twitches with impatience as he waits for his food to be served. The staff here, he concludes, are just as sullen, inefficient and uncaring as his own servants and womenfolk. In his mind's eye, he recalls his wedding photo in which he stands proud and young, at the age of seventeen. Next to him is his 15-year-old bride, who later bore him six children.

Now, as a highly successful businessman who provides for his family's every need, he cannot understand why he is refused the respect he feels he deserves. It is no wonder that he lingers in the glamorous film world where he has played a major and extremely ruthless business role. As for women, he often seeks his pleasure elsewhere, even if it has resulted in contracting diseases which he then transfers to his wife. When his daughters reproach him, he shouts until they leave. He performs his religious *puja* devotions every day, convinced that this reduces any 'bad' karma.

A year later he is lying in bed, so crippled by disease that he can barely move. At first, he vents his anger, as usual, on his servants. His daughters, assuming that he is now receiving just punishment for his vices, decide to keep well away. In this state of semi-isolation, the man has much time to ponder, to regret his radical actions and sharp tongue. He realises that even in this state of utter helplessness, he still has a choice. While he may not be able to choose his actions on a physical plane, he can choose his words, and so he speaks to the servants in a less aggressive tone. He can no longer enjoy the riches he has accumulated, but he can bestow them on others.

Instructing his servants to write a long letter of explanation and apology to his daughters, he tells them about his years of frustration and loneliness. In turn, they are moved by this unexpected expression of his feelings. The picture they have entertained for decades of their father as a selfish philanderer slowly crumbles. They realise that judgments based on incomplete Information have no validity and they understand that all the seemingly negative aspects of their father's life may have been necessary for this one supreme moment of reconciliation when they approach his bedside after years of mutual animosity.

Questions

How quick are you to judge?
Which relationships in your life need healing?

Suppose 'healing' is just a matter of becoming more aware or communicating more?
Suppose there are more choices available to you in difficult situations than you think?
Have activities leading to financial gain impaired your sensitivity to others?
How do you choose to react to long-term criticism from close relatives?
To what degree is your picture of yourself determined by the opinion of others?

How would you regard people with extreme views differently, if you realised their soul's agenda is to use all possible means to elicit a response, shocking an unconscious, passive, violent world into the realisation that love is the only answer?

What if everyone in the world who has experienced pain were able to move towards reconciliation?

GLOBAL VILLAGER 26: OMNIPRESENCE

Man aged 25 from Delhi, India. Buddhist, lives in poverty and is undernourished, literate, speaks Hindi

A dark, red wall hides all but the tip of a very large, white building resembling a flower stretching into the sky. Unaware of the presence of this building, a sour-faced young man crouches in front of the wall. As he stares into the distance, he seems far removed from the bustle of Delhi's streets, the honking taxis and the strains of Bollywood music blaring out from hundreds of cassette recorders. However, it is here that he squats and waits, on the cobbled pavement, waiting for his next customer's shoes to appear before him to be polished. He rarely looks at their faces, but often sneaks a furtive look at their erotic-looking women. When he is not working, his eyes are free to rove. When he sees women shopping in their flamboyantly coloured saris and sporting bare midriffs, he tries to hide the dull, hot flush which flows through him. Occasionally, in the evenings, he suddenly becomes aware of an acute emptiness which he is desperate to fill, and it is all he can do to prevent himself assaulting some young woman down a back street. When he arrives home he furtively looks at photos of nude women which he hides under his mattress. On days where he has earned more money than usual, he chews on a betel nut to ease his pain and his unfulfilled sexual longings.

One morning as he squats on the pavement, he suddenly senses that the wall behind him has some sort of oppressive power, caging his freedom, separating him from something important. Seized by a feeling of intense curiosity, the man wonders why he has never climbed the wall before. On the other side, he sees a huge, white temple built like a giant lotus flower. As he walks slowly towards it, he feels increasingly aware of every tiny physical sensation around him. Inside the Lotus Baha'i Temple, he finds members of all religions meditating together, and all holy scripts are laid out in their original languages without translations or interpretations. When he re-enters the bright sunlight, it is as if his emptiness has been replaced by a fire of energy which burns within him and stretches to touch every living creature within sight. For a moment, he can physically feel the footsteps of the pilgrims at the gateway, as if they are walking on his skin. And at that same moment, he understands that he is inseparable from the earth's crust and that he is present in ALL. He thanks the lotus goddess, Lakshmi, for the discovery of his cosmic self.

Customers start to come to him on a regular basis because they sense his interest, sensitivity and compassion. The man's ability to connect with the needs of other people as well as the needs of his own body increases dramatically. No longer ashamed of his sexual impulses, he attracts a woman well versed in the tantric tradition, with whom he can connect on all levels – emotional, spiritual and sexual. As his inner awareness grows, he develops a sharp eye for his fellow beings and dedicates himself to humanity as a whole.

Questions

What are you secretly longing to do?
Which emotions are you hiding? What lies beyond the wall?
What do you not want to see? How long are you going to wait?
When you reach a state of pure energy, what will you do first?
What can you do to express your sexuality more fully?
Are you aware of any unexpressed, pent-up aggression which might lead you – in a sudden eruption of feeling – to endanger yourself or another person?
Supposing we are all one, capable of communicating on every level and with everything?
What would change if everyone was allowed to worship in any sacred place they liked, however they wanted? What place is not sacred and who does not belong to the cosmic self?
What if everyone worldwide knew that real happiness is a side effect of dedicating ourselves to a cause larger than ourselves?

GLOBAL VILLAGER 27: IMMORTALITY

Woman aged 70 from Varanasi, India. Hindu, lives in poverty
and is undernourished, illiterate, speaks Hindi

A woman sits motionless on the pavement with her beggar's
bowl, focusing on the rubbish-filled road. Behind her is the hovel
she sleeps in. Above her are the tangle of power cables deliver-
ing electricity to unknown destinations. Her thin, green shawl covers her emaciated body as much as possible. She is resigned
to her surroundings and does not want to move. She does not
contemplate going to the Holy Ganges to wash, although it is not
far to go, because she fears the pain in her limbs whenever she
starts to walk. Her nearness to death is also a source of fear. She
envies the children with their energy and quick, painless movement, and she grumbles at all the travellers who do not seem to
see her begging bowl. Turning her attention to those who are
even worse off than herself, she comforts herself with the thought
that they are going to die first.

During unusually heavy rain, the woman crouches in her hovel,
looking up for the first time in several years, anxious that the
power cables might fall upon her. Beyond the cables she sees a
light and suddenly recognizes that it comes from the Observation
Tower which she climbed as a girl – a place to look at and interpret the stars. Here she is in Varanasi, the City of Light, where
she grew up as a child. Here, her journey has turned a full circle.

The woman's anger at the passing travellers now dissipates as
she realizes that most of them are on a spiritual quest, seeking
out the City of Light to connect to the heavens. As dawn breaks,
she begins to perform traditional rites of worship, and though she
is aware of pain as she slowly descends to bathe in the holy waters, it is not foremost in her consciousness. As she washes herself in the river, she simultaneously cleanses herself and her
mind of all fear.

Suddenly she is fully convinced of the immortality of her soul. Instead of lamenting, she looks forward in anticipation to the life which she will create next. The woman remembers her mother telling her about the Hindu belief that time occurs in cosmic cycles of 12,000 divine years, and she feels that she is an intrinsic part of these cycles. Her relaxed face and smiling eyes ensure that passers-by drop money into her bowl from time to time. This she shares with those less fortunate than herself. She is blessed by their gratitude and companionship until it is time for her to move on into the next life.

Questions

What are you begging for?
What if your soul were immortal?
What if you did not compare your own experience to others?
If you get what you want, are you sure you will be completely content?
Is your focus primarily on those who have more or less than yourself?
How many of your actions are dictated by fear and how could your greatest fear be an indicator of where to go next?
How would you live life differently if you knew for certain that we are creating every second of your reality with each thought you think and each decision you make?
What will change if you believed that every generous action you take returns to you in some form?
What if death (and the death of every new experience) were the beginning of a breathtakingly wonderful new experience?
What if everyone throughout the world conducted their lives in full knowledge of the fact that everything always comes to an end which is followed by a new beginning, and that our soul / our essence is eternal?
What if everyone worldwide viewed their life on this planet as a temporary stage in their continuing evolution and as part of an eternal divine cycle?

GLOBAL VILLAGER 28: SELF DISCIPLINE

Man aged 46 from near Hyderabad, India. Muslim, lives in poverty and is undernourished, literate, speaks Dakhini

It is early morning in the Char Minar district of Hyderabad, and a man is still asleep on his threadbare mat. As on every morning during Ramadan, he is woken by drums which signal the possibility to have a pre-dawn meal. The wealthy Muslim families donate food at this time of year. This is why the man has walked to Hyderabad from his rural village. He does not feel part of the city itself with its bustle, traffic snarls and opulent fruit markets, from which he is sorely tempted to steal. But he reprimands himself for this thought. Generally, he continues to struggle along his structured and well-worn paths of conditioned behaviour and stunted aspiration, hoping that somehow, he will be able to pull himself together and actively combat his poverty.

On this particular morning, during a period of semi-consciousness, he dreams of a god who resembles a man and a lion simultaneously. When the drums sound, he wakes to a curious feeling of displacement, but he is also strangely energised. During his wanderings through the city he finds an old wizened man who has been meditating under the same tree for 60 years, so that the tree has grown around him. In another street, he sees an Aghora yogi meditating on top of a rubbish heap. The man is shocked, convinced that they must be mad. He is sure he can never achieve peace of mind through such practices, and he certainly cannot uphold the necessary self-discipline.

As the man walks around Hyderabad, he passes the bus station where several excursions are on offer for pilgrims and tourists. He is astonished to see a poster depicting the lion-man of his dream and he feels strangely compelled to find out more. This is Narasimha, an incarnation of Vishnu, the life preserver. When he hears about the sacred Narasimha temple not far away, with its ability to enlighten the 'darkened' mind, the man feels instinctively impelled to make a pilgrimage to this Hindu shrine, despite his Muslim beliefs. On his way to the cave he is impressed by the discipline of the poorer pilgrims who fold their clothes with extreme care before donning white robes. Like generations of sages before him, intending to access their own inherent power, the man touches the rock archway of the cave and feels a blast of energy blowing away his old conditioning. From this new perspective, the 'madmen' meditating under trees or on rubbish tips are no longer insane, but saints following their own chosen path to self-realization. He realizes that everyone can chose their own path towards self-improvement and spirituality. Consciously and methodically, he starts his own journey towards enlightenment, realizing that in his particular case, self-discipline is a major key.

Questions

How seriously do you take your dreams?
Can you identify new sources of energy for yourself?
What rituals can you embrace to access your own power?
Which areas of your life would benefit from more discipline?
What if we all recognised the truths at the core of every religion?

Which well-worn path do you find difficult to leave, although you recognise the necessity?
What if enlightenment is not only a 60-year journey but also a decision you can make today?
Are you aware that all dreams are in your grasp if you move towards them step by step?
What appears to be shocking, but is actually the result of your own conditioning?
How does comparing yourself to others decrease or increase your momentum to change?
What if everyone worldwide respected everyone else's chosen path?

GLOBAL VILLAGER 29: UNIQUENESS

Woman aged 25 from Uttar Pradesh, India. Muslim, lives in poverty and is undernourished, literate, speaks Hindi

A woman sits inside her home and cries in one of the rare moments which she has to herself. Her mind is completely blocked. She no longer knows who she is. On the surface, it still looks as if she is the wife of a rickshaw puller and the mother of four children, living in a dusty, pot-holed, Muslim-dominated town which has suffered decades of neglect. But underneath she feels she is no-one, with no voice to protest and no hands to act. Although she suffers greatly, she does not dare to tell anyone that she has been raped by her father-in-law. When he feels it is time, her father-in-law, as head of the family, makes it public. He insists he has absolute authority and has told her she must move in with him. The village council confirms that – under the Shariat and by Islamic law – she must become the wife of her rapist and treat her husband as her son. Despite her overwhelming inner pain and turmoil, she agrees because she does not want to be accused of betraying her faith.

When the woman's heels start to throb with unbearable pain, she knows intuitively that she must run and make a complete break for the sake of her four confused daughters, as well as herself. This is a pivotal moment in her life. She wrenches herself from everything she has ever known, packs her bags and escapes with her family. Her previous life disintegrates. She is on the brink of new structures, in defiance of centuries of expectations and ancient memory patterns which dictate female submission.

Soon she is living with relatives in a completely different part of the country where no one can find her. Here, religious laws carry little momentum compared with humanitarian principles, and the woman feels as if she has entered paradise. Her mental landscape undergoes great changes as she emerges from being a submissive, all-obedient underdog into a confident, independent woman who is often in the public eye. She manages to regard the horrific circumstances of yesterday with detachment and see them as a painful but necessary part of her awakening. With time, she even feels grateful for the experience which forced her combat her own feeling of insignificance and which led her to the conviction that she, like all other human beings, is absolutely unique.

Questions

Is it time to run?
Can you let go?
Are you a victim?
Do you know who you are?
Where do you want to go to?
In what sense are you 'headless'?
How good are you at setting limits?
Are you neglecting yourself for others?
Do you recognise the importance of determining your destination before deciding who to travel with?
Do you recognise the danger of choosing your travelling companions first?
How much personal responsibility do you abdicate to authority, religious or otherwise?
Which part of yourself are you allowing to be completely disregarded or 'raped'?
What dreadful event is showing you that it is in the interest of your higher self to change direction?
To what extent do you see life as movement?
Are you moving through ever higher stages of awareness?
What would change in your life if you were convinced of your own uniqueness?

What if we all focussed on the inspirational core truths of our religions rather than adhering to their rules?

GLOBAL VILLAGER 30: SELF ASSERTION

Woman aged 43 from Bombay, India. Hindu, lives in poverty and is undernourished, beaten, has unsafe drinking water, illiterate, speaks Marathi

A tired woman rests for a moment, leaning against a stack of bricks. Dust is caught in the folds of her faded sari and in the wrinkles around her eyes. She bends down to heave the bricks she has made into a wooden cart. A torn cloth covers her head, protecting her from the fierce sun and framing her lined face which is usually turned towards the ground. As one of India's 160 million 'untouchables' – people too impure to rank as a human being – she is universally despised. As she works, she pushes away memories of her small house and chickens outside Bombay which she was forced to leave. The other villagers criticised her for doing business which was unsuited to her lowly station. They killed her poultry, stripped off her clothes, jeered at her and banned her to the edges of the village. Now, in the city, she sporadically finds menial labour, but sometimes she is forced to beg, squatting at the roadside and holding out her metal bowl. While she hates the upper classes for their vile treatment of her, she is resigned to the fact that this is her karma: she is being punished for misdeeds in her previous life.

When she arrives very early at the quarry one morning, she sees an unfamiliar figure in the distance, moving around energetically from one worker to the next. She also sees an unfamiliar object – a tall black stand with something on top of it. As the man comes closer and closer, the woman becomes increasingly tense, pulling her scarf in front of her face, turning away in fear and engrossing herself in her work. Finally, he is standing right next to her. Although she does not acknowledge him, he explains who he is. He makes documentary films: he would like her permission to film her at the quarry and to document the lives of 'untouchables' because they have no voice of their own. When she hears these kind words from the mouth of a complete stranger who seems to be so concerned about the fate of her own kind, she bursts into tears, remembering the terrible scenes as she was forced to leave her village. Everyone else deserted her. The man is appalled that he has upset her and asks what he can do to help. Despite the urge to hide her shame, the woman courageously breaks new ground and tells the man everything. The film crew accompanies her back to the village, and her story becomes part of the documentary.

The villagers know this and express their deep regret. To make amends, they reinstate her into the village and society in general. Henceforth, the village becomes extremely popular because it is known as a place where the caste system does not operate. Everyone has equal opportunities. The woman herself is conscious of her own great power and no longer implicitly accepts those limitations set by people who consider themselves on a higher level. She realises that God, or Spirit, or the Divine Energy, is not a force which issues punishment if specific requirements are not met. Now, with each footstep, she carefully carves her own way forward, aware that she is the sole creator of every moment.

Questions

Who would listen to your story?
How often do you resign to 'fate'?
How have you deserted yourself?
How are you punishing yourself?
Are you what people say you are?
What is your first instinct when you are presented with something new?
How deep is your awareness of the fact that you are the sole creator of every moment?
What if you accept that whatever trait you despise in another is exactly the trait you despise in yourself?
What if everyone worldwide trained their ability to love?
What if everyone worldwide respected each other?

GLOBAL VILLAGER 31: PARTICIPATION

Boy aged 5 from Jharkhand, India. Hindu, lives in poverty and is undernourished, illiterate, stunted growth, has unsafe drinking water, speaks Bengali

A small, twisted figure is sleeping in a grey cardboard box. The boy was born into a tiny village hemmed in by hills, near a large uranium mine, and he is so stunted that it is hard to believe that he is five years old. Born with only one eye and bent legs, he cannot stand. A large part of his day is spent sitting on a mat inside, playing with a stick or ball of earth. His mother keeps him well away from the other villagers, despite her son's protests. She is worried that the other children will make fun of him and she feels great shame at his deformities. Although she imagines that this is somehow part of her karma, something deep inside her rebels against this explanation. Together with all the other women she walks towards the local pond which serves as drinking and washing water. Like the others she pretends not to see the putrid, stinking debris at its edges, and like the others she worries about her husband in the mine, working without any protection and inhaling poisonous uranium dust.

One morning as the boy's mother approaches the river with her washing, she finds all the other women running in the opposite direction, their faces torn with fear. There has been a serious accident in the mine. The mother discovers that a member of her extended family has been killed. Overcome with grief, she decides that the only way to pull her life together is to seek advice from a relative who is a spiritual healer in the distant city of Patna. Reluctantly she puts her deformed son under the protection of a nearby farmer.

Suddenly the boy is exposed to the light and surrounded by other children. At this point he understands the meaning of loneliness and attempts to ease this by offering friendship to other 'lost' boys on the edge of the village community. Slowly, he integrates himself into daily village life. His active participation as well as his appearance has a profound effect on his onlookers. His continued presence in the public eye forces others to reassess their attitudes and go into action. Later in life, he decides to exhibit his deformity as proof of uranium pollution in the region. This leads to great changes and healthier living conditions in the village. His mother has long since accepted that there is a level of experience where every condition and circumstance is perfect for any one person at any one time.

Questions

What do you consider as "normal"?
Which area of your life is in stagnation?
How much do you worry about appearances?
Is there anyone who you are trying to protect?
What gut feeling or what 'poison' are you ignoring?
What if your protection means stunting their development?
Is there anything you are hiding which you are ashamed of?

Which of your emotions would you describe as 'stunted'
or 'under-developed'?

How desperate does a situation have to be before you
go into action?

What if you believed that there is a valid reason for all
unpleasant occurrences?

What if every person – however deformed or obnoxious or
unpleasant, and however coincidental the meeting - has a
specific and perfect message for you which fits in with your
soul's agenda, and what if everyone looked beyond
unpleasant circumstances to see that everything is
always perfect for their spiritual advance?

GLOBAL VILLAGER 32: ALERTNESS

Woman aged 24 from Punjab, India. Hindu, lives in poverty, is undernourished, unsafe drinking water, literate, speaks Hindi

The huge concrete square in the city of Chandigarh is dotted with groups of people talking, selling, or going about their daily business. A woman walks slowly across it, carrying a load of wood on her head. She concentrates on balancing the weight, and her eyes focus on the other end of the square which is lined with imposing buildings. These were designed in the fifties by the French architect Le Corbusier. Though she is very familiar with these buildings, she has disliked them ever since her childhood, resenting the way a foreigner has forced his presence upon Chandigarh in such an insensitive way. Now the buildings look even worse because the humid climate has taken its toll: the metalwork has rusted and there are visible cracks in the concrete. Le Corbusier's huge sculpture of a right hand stretches randomly into a metallic sky.

When she arrives at her makeshift home, a tent made of scrap material, she tries to make a fire but the wood is damp. She feels that everything is rotting, including herself. Succumbing to overwhelming tiredness, she cries herself to sleep, convinced that if she disappeared from the face of the earth, nobody would notice.

During the night, the woman dreams that she is wearing tight, uncomfortable clothes and biting her lips. She is walking endlessly along a narrow path towards a beautiful tall tower, but when she arrives, it is actually a crumbling ruin. Confused, she looks around to see where she has come from. The narrow path stretches far away into the distance. To her horror, she can also see what she has missed – turnings to the right and left leading to idyllic fields and rivers. The woman awakes the next morning in a state of shock. She is sure that the dream is trying to tell her something. In a state of extreme alertness, she conducts her daily chores, and though this is her normal routine, everything is different. Again, she walks across the square with her firewood. Aware of an oncoming headache, she decides to carry the wood on her back instead, leaving her head free to move in all directions and to see everything which she usually overlooks – the resilient weeds pushing through minute cracks, the tiny darting lizards between her feet and the birds in the sky. Instead of directing her thoughts towards the crumbling architecture at its edges, she now actively participates in the lively bustle of activity in the middle of the square, greeting acquaintances energetically, responding positively to their invitations and suggestions.

She realises that she is now allowing her rigid behavioural structures and inflexibility to crumble, and she is full of enthusiasm for her new life in exactly the same place, Chandigarh. For this empowered woman, there is suddenly great significance in the fact that the city is named after Chandi, the goddess of power. Instead of rejecting Chandigarh's foreign architecture, the woman rejoices every time she passes, viewing it as the fulfilment of one man's vision. Le Corbusier's sculpture, the huge right hand, reminds her to be alert to opportunity and 'handle' her own future.

Questions

In what way do you feel you are surrounded by things which are 'foreign', 'different', 'incomprehensible' or 'wrong'?
Could this be nothing more than your viewpoint?
Given that we are all one, who would be a foreigner?
How deeply do you believe that we are all wholly responsible for what we choose to look at and how we choose to look at it?
What is so obvious that it is being overlooked?
How actively do you participate in life around you?
Are you aware that you control your own future?
Given that we are all gods and goddesses with divine power, what vision will you turn into reality?
What if everyone worldwide paid close attention to their dreams understood their message?

GLOBAL VILLAGER 33: DIVINITY

Girl aged 2 from Calcutta, India. Hindu, lives in poverty and is undernourished, stunted growth, speaks Hindi

On the banks of the Hooghly River in Calcutta, a small child is being wrapped lovingly by her mother in the only clothes she has. When she was a starving new-born baby and when her bones were still soft, her arms were twisted by her mother so that, later, she would be able to earn more money as a beggar. The sight of her deformed limbs impels passers-by to be more generous, and so her deformity keeps both of them alive.

The child is not so aware of its deformity. It is generally happy in the secure knowledge that it is greatly loved and will be sung to sleep every night. It also knows, on a completely different level, that its purpose on earth is to initiate the first stage in her mother's soul agenda – to experience giving love and comfort – but that it must leave again to enable her Mother to go on to the second stage – spreading compassion on a much larger scale.

Although the child dies of diphtheria, the child's soul can still speak to her mother in her hour of deepest despair. She instructs her to take her old baby clothes to 'Mother's House' in Calcutta, and to never stop singing.

Despite her great grief, the woman hears and heeds the inner voice which speaks to her and wanders the streets in search of a hostel which looks after deprived mothers, but she is unsuccessful. Then she remembers to sing, and intuition takes her to her destination, 'Mother's House'.

However, this is not a refuge for destitute mothers, but a house run by a mother. She walks through the gates singing, joining all the other people who simply turn up to help the ill and dying. No one is turned away. The sound of her beautiful voice is a joy and comfort to all the patients in her care. She has a roof over her head and enough to eat. Her gratitude is great, and she needs no more, fulfilled by touching the lives of so many.

She is eternally grateful to her daughter who first inspired her to love and to sing, and she knows that her daughter is an angel with a divine purpose.

Questions

Do you value the gentle innocence, enthusiasm and unconditional love demonstrated by small children?
How could you become more like them?
What if it were impossible for your life to be meaningless?
How can you assist others to develop their potential?

Can you accept that you are a certain 'stage' in everyone else's life (and that they are a stage in yours) for a specific purpose?

Are you aware that you are an angel and that your appearance on this earth, as well as your death, occurs at the perfect moment and has a particular meaning for all concerned?

Are you aware that we are all angels in this respect?

What if death is not death but the beginning of a new life and purpose which you can decide?

Can you contemplate the possibility that before you entered this life, you agreed to endure certain sufferings on this earth so that you and your fellow beings could experience something which is of crucial importance to you all?

What if everyone worldwide were aware of their own divinity and purpose?

GLOBAL VILLAGER 34: COMPASSION

Woman aged 25 from Calcutta, India. Hindu, lives in poverty and is undernourished, illiterate, speaks Hindi

Surrounded by piles of pungent rubbish, a mother dresses her child in the only clothes it has. They are long enough to cover its deliberately deformed limbs. Soon the woman will sing her daughter to sleep and they will spend the night together, as they spend every night, on a patch of hard concrete near the Hooghly river in Calcutta.

Every morning the woman smears her face and stringy hair with dirt, hides her daughter's clothes and takes her to the city with her begging bowl. There she sits on the pavement, displaying the child naked to invoke the sympathy of passers-by. Often, she deeply regrets the permanent damage which she has inflicted upon her daughter, but sometimes she is simply glad that this has saved both of them from definite starvation.

When the child dies of diphtheria, her mother wants to die too. For a while, she continues to sing to the clothes her daughter used to wear. Then she walks like a ghost through the streets of Calcutta. In the course of her wanderings she overhears two women talking, saying that they want to go "Mother House". At exactly the same moment, the distraught mother hears an inner voice, urging her to take her dead daughter's clothes there, and insisting that she should not stop singing.

The woman stops sobbing and starts to look for a hostel which takes in deprived mothers, but she is unsuccessful. Then she re-members that the voice told her to sing, and so she continues her search singing. At last she finds 'Mother's House", where she is immediately welcomed.

This is a hostel founded by a mother to help the poor and the woman joins all the other people who simply turn up to help the ill and dying. No-one is turned away. The sound of her beautiful voice is a joy and comfort to all the patients in her care. She has a roof over her head and enough to eat. Her compassion is great, and she needs no more, fulfilled by touching the lives of so many.

She teaches the Mandala of Great Compassion to all those who suffer. Like Avalokiteshvara, holding 1,000 eyes in 1,000 hands, she witnesses the sufferings of others. During meditation, she envisages herself at the core of a huge mandala, sending energy to every suffering being worldwide with every breath.

Questions

What if you are always forgiven?
What method do you use to invoke sympathy?
How often are your decisions motivated by love?
How often are your decisions motivated by fear?
Is there someone you can forgive, including yourself?
Which part of yourself have you disfigured or distorted?
Could you be looking for the wrong thing in the wrong place?

What has 'died', and how does this "death" open up new perspectives for you?

Have you contemplated expressing yourself more through music?

What if your need to be comforted is healed by comforting others?

What if everyone treated everyone as members of the same family, showing compassion at every opportunity?

GLOBAL VILLAGER 35: ABILITY TO LISTEN

Woman aged 19 from Moscow, Russia.
Hindu, literate, speaks Russian

A young woman runs her fingers slowly across her lips. They feel strangely numb, as if her mouth has been sewn up for a very long time. As a child, she was intimidated and rigidly controlled by her parents, and her chosen reaction to this was stubborn silence.

Now, as a young woman, she is fascinated by the Hare Krishna movement, of which she has become a fanatical member. She rebels against her disapproving family, hurting others with her fanaticism, rejecting anyone who fails to show similar enthusiasm. She points her finger accusingly at those in positions of power and is proud to belong to a movement which is different. At work, in her badly paid job serving in a café, she is sullen and outspoken. She is in danger of losing her job because she sometimes alienates the guests.

One day, a tourist enters the café on a hot sweltering day. For some reason, she is the only guest at that time. The woman tourist sits down and immediately takes out a postcard of a white church standing in flooded meadows – the Russian Church of the Intercession on the River Nerl.

The moment the waitress sees the postcard of the church, she is strangely struck by its beautiful simplicity and pure structure. Suddenly, she realises that this too can be a spiritual home and inspiration for others, even if it is not her own. Instead of gruffly asking for her order, the waitress greets the tourist with spontaneous warmth, her face shining, her heart open. Their mutual enthusiasm for the church on the postcard is the start of a new friendship.

The girl realises that every newcomer to the café presents her with a new opportunity to listen, to encounter a plethora of different wishes, views, habits and beliefs. Her ears are finely attuned to everything and everyone around her. Her tolerance grows, learning that there are many valid paths towards positive change. Insisting that others follow her own rigid ideals was often tantamount to condemnation, or an attempt to control.

The young woman ceases to blame her superiors or people in positions of power for her own situation, taking on responsibility instead.

Questions

What need fuels your urge to be different?
How has fanaticism made you less tolerant?
Is speaking your mind an action or a reaction?
Is it an attempt to control others?
What if your behaviour is less reaction and more self-chosen?
Suppose you spent one day without criticizing or complaining?

Have there been long periods when you have kept your silence?

How much responsibility for yourself do you abdicate to a group or to those in positions of power?

What if everyone – regardless of their religion – treated everyone else with careful consideration and tolerance in complete awareness of the fact that all paths lead to "heaven"?

What if everyone worldwide exercised religious tolerance?

GLOBAL VILLAGER 36:
WELCOMING THE NEW

Woman aged 35 from Moscow, Russia. Christian, literate, pregnant, sexually abused, speaks Russian

An attractive Russian woman in her mid-thirties is sitting on her bed, wondering what to do next. She has discovered, yet again, that she is pregnant and is contemplating whether to have another abortion. It would be her ninth. Contraceptives are expensive and difficult to get hold of, and she does not want to refuse the attention of her lover. She feels very guilty, due to her Christian upbringing. How wonderful it would be to play again like to a small child with no responsibilities or difficult choices, running around with her friends on Moscow's huge Red Square, just a short walk from her home. She hates the decision-making process and feels very much alone. She is sure that her lover has no interest in raising a family and will leave her if she says she wants to keep the baby.

Still uncertain of what to do, she spontaneously decides to visit her old childhood neighbourhood in the hope of gaining some clarity of thought. As she crosses Red Square, she hears American tourists exclaiming with great surprise to learn that 'Red' Square has nothing to do with Communism, but with the red wall around the Kremlin. Red, in fact, means beautiful. The woman is struck by the fact that something can suddenly be seen completely differently, and that there are always new paths to pursue.

Wondering how this might apply to her own life, she re-examines her own behaviour and eventually realises that having abortions is not a bid for personal freedom but a method of shunning responsibility. She also realises that her previous abortions have left emotional scars which she has ignored. Fear of the future has prevented her from welcoming new experiences into her life, including children. Taking all her courage in her hands, she decides that this time, she will keep the baby and turn her life in a new direction, taking only those things with her which she is really passionate about. She does not let financial considerations – or her fear of survival – influence her decision to keep this child.

When she tells her lover, he is surprised but reacts with joy. Could she really have misjudged him so completely? Resolving to talk much more about her hopes and fears in future, a rush of energy, like sap rising in a young plant, moves up through her body. Inwardly, she caresses the new life which is growing in her womb.

Questions

Could you communicate your hopes and fears more?
What new experience are you not allowing into your life?
What role does the feeling of responsibility play in your life?
How often are your choices determined by existential or survival or financial fears?
Suppose guilt is sometimes the result of overstepping limits set by others?
What qualities do small children demonstrate so easily and which ones would you like to acquire again?
Are you surrounded by things and people you are passionate about? If not, why not?
Are you aware that you learn the most when you enter a new, unknown zone?
Do you rejoice in the ultimate possibilities that each day provides anew?

What will happen when everyone finds the courage to break away from old structures, welcoming new opportunities and experiences into their lives?

GLOBAL VILLAGER 37: COMMITMENT

Man aged 50 from Ekaterinburg, Russia, non-religious, literate, overweight, smokes, drinks, speaks Russian

A rather shaky hand is delving into a fat wallet to find some money. It belongs to a plump Russian man with a worried look on his face. Quickly, he gives the money to his small nephew, saying he is sorry to have forgotten his birthday. The man tends to feel 'weak' when confronted with angry children, or indeed with any strong emotions, preferring to solve problems of this nature with money rather than considering his role in creating them.

For him, money is a useful way of expressing affection – a viable alternative to personal commitment. His greatest wish is to feel secure, and his greatest fear is that the money he owns could actually become worthless. Firmly cemented in the physical and material world, he is very cynical about anything which suggests that there are other non-physical or spiritual realms. As far as he is concerned, death is the end of life and something he tries not to think about. But despite his outward nonchalance, death secretly haunts him. His shaking hand betrays his fear of spending, and his life lacks all sense of enjoyment.

Scouring the newspaper for financial news and trends, the man reads about a Siberian farmer who is filing the state for damages and who is in fear of his life. The farmer was nearly hit several times by rocket debris returning to earth from space. This seriously impairs the man's feelings of security. Despite any measures he may take to protect himself on earth, financial or otherwise, he realises that he cannot control debris from space.

This thought impels him to look up at the sky anxiously whenever he is out walking, and he is overcome with a sense of helplessness. Simultaneously, a crash in the financial markets forces him to reconsider what is of real lasting value to himself. He realises that paradise is not a place of security or a full bank account, but a state of mind. He gains an understanding of why he is on this earth, and realises that the material world is a temporary aspect of his present experience, which is a short sojourn in an eternal spiritual quest. He now knows that new life begins with the destruction of old forms, and that this is a continual process of building on strengths and reviewing weaknesses. He commits to every new person who enters his life in the knowledge that they will provide him with an opportunity to grow. His greatest joy is spending time with his small nieces and nephews who infect him with their spontaneity and enthusiasm, and his greatest gift to them is the interest which he shows in their lives.

Questions

To what extent are you cynical?
What role does money play in your life?
What is of real genuine, lasting value?
What prevents you from entering true intimacy?
Is it time to discover your very specific purpose in life?
Do you tend to use money more for things or experiences?
Do you build on your strengths and review your weaknesses?

What if there are always new realms and experiences open to us, providing we open our eyes and believe that they are possible?

What if everyone worldwide realised that new beginnings ensue from the destruction of old forms?

How would the world change if everyone maintained a high level of authenticity in all relationships?

GLOBAL VILLAGER 38: INTENSITY

Girl aged 16 from Bangladesh. Muslim, illiterate, speaks Bengali

A young woman is dreaming of having a child. She visualises herself as a beautiful bride, and then as a glowing mother-to-be with a baby growing inside her. In her mind's eye, she sees red and purple cells magically dividing and re-dividing. However, her dreams are in vain, as she has no chance of experiencing this. Her face is half covered by a veil to hide her discoloured, scarred skin. An acid attack was her punishment for refusing to accept an admirer's proposal of marriage. Her appearance is something she cannot change, and she has resigned herself to the childless, uneventful life of a social outcast. Although she stands by her decision, she is also overcome by remorse. If she goes out in public, people will stare at her and her family will be in disgrace. Perhaps she would even endanger the marriage opportunities of her younger sisters. This is why she prefers to hide herself from the public eye, closeted in the stuffy, cramped family home. She dreams of running about outside, the wind on her face.

When she overhears her father discussing future husbands for her younger sisters without their knowledge, the girl is wrought with despair, wondering if they will agree or have to endure the same fate as herself. Summoning all her courage, she leaves the house in secret and searches for help. When she discovers a centre for the rehabilitation of acid victims, she is able to follow her own path without compromising her family.

With time, the girl's focus is no longer on her outward appearance. Her soul's agenda is to go within and to discover other qualities and skills. She experiments increasingly and launches into such an intense period of creativity and learning that her scars are forgotten and her face is radiant with energy and joy. Realising that this experience and the full, exciting life she now leads would not have been possible if she had become a well-behaved and duteous bride at the age of sixteen, she is thankful for the incident – however dreadful – which cut off that option, thus opening up completely new avenues. She is now aware of her basic rights as a woman and as a human being, and she immediately helps anyone who is denied their rights. While assisting the Adibashi community to voice their complaints against land loss, she develops a sense of family belonging with other activists, including her future husband. Whenever opportunity arises, she meditates alone, standing in the wind, her arms pointing towards the sky, filled with an intense exuberance and the knowledge that everything is possible.

Questions

What is on your soul's agenda?
What would you like to give birth to?

Will you change your situation or are you going to wait until some unpleasant incident forces you to take a new direction?

Are you aware of the miracle that growth and creativity are always possible in every area of life and "death"?

How strong is your feeling of responsibility to others,
thus abdicating responsibility for yourself?

What if people who commit violence are (on a completely different level) carrying out a divine plan to make us reassess ourselves and move up to a higher level of consciousness?

How would the world change if everyone were capable of leaving bitter disappointment behind them?

How would the world change if everyone focussed on entering into a new intensive stage of life,
leading to fulfilment on all levels?

GLOBAL VILLAGER 39: COURAGE

Girl aged 11 from Manila, the Philippines. Christian,
lives in poverty and is undernourished, literate,
works full time, speaks Filipino

The pile of clean, wet clothes increases rapidly as a small girl deftly washes the laundry in a plastic bowl. She works full time as a domestic help for a large family in Manila. Her employers deny her the right to education, but her dearest wish is to go to secondary school in the countryside where she comes from. Any pay she receives immediately goes to her poverty-stricken mother who lives in the slums of Manila. Work starts at 5 o'clock every morning and sometimes she is called out in the middle of the night. She is overburdened with duties and beaten if she does not complete them. On several occasions, she has been severely whipped. Now – which is even worse – her employer has threatened to sever her contact to her mother. Exhausted and abused, she feels like she is in hell, like a helpless being living in a shed with no light. The washing seems to be more important than herself, as it requires more water than she is allowed to use to wash herself. The pigs she looks after also eat better than she does. Most of the time, she has the strange feeling she is invisible, feeling more like an old woman than a young girl. On the other hand, she knows that running away and begging on the streets is a dangerous practise, as patrols regularly 'rescue' street children and throw them into prison.

After a particularly busy week, the girl cries constantly due to exhaustion and – in her desperation – she screams at her employers that she needs sleep, food and water just like they do. Her employers are surprised by this sudden, uncharacteristic outburst which has the ring of truth about it, and so they give her a day off to recover. But the ill-treatment continues. Gradually, the girl realises that feeling invisible is the result of acting as if she really were invisible, always towing the line. Now she dares to confide in her mother about being abused. Her mother, in turn, informs social workers who tell her about laws preventing child exploitation. The girl is brought to a safe haven, a community providing shelter, food and counselling. Instead of hovering in the background, the girl regains self-confidence and learns to shine, spreading her light everywhere she goes. She realises that her transformation was only made possible by her experience of "darkness". She moves forward through the various stages of her life with unflinching courage, serving as a luminous example to others in distress.

Questions

Which duty do you continue to carry out, despite it being detrimental to your health?

What would change if you were your first priority?

In what areas of your life do you feel invisible and to what extent is this just your view?

What if the experience of 'darkness' is one of the greatest paths to illumination and transformation?

Which secret still needs to be confided?

What fear prevents you from exploring new avenues of help?

How do we contribute to our own feeling that we are in 'hell'?

What if we were all meant to shine and inspire,
and if we all believed that we had the ability to do so, filling the world with peace and light?

GLOBAL VILLAGER 40:
SPIRIT OF ADVENTURE

Girl aged 7 from the banks of the Mekong, Laos. Christian, lives in poverty, is undernourished, illiterate, speaks Lahu

A child walks listlessly along the sandy banks of the Mekong River, clutching a banana. Unlike the other children who pick up pebbles from the banks to throw into the water, she walks past them with a glazed look of disinterest, avoiding their eyes. Even when the other children suddenly scream with excitement, rushing towards a woman in a boat who distributes small parcels, she automatically turns away. In fact, she considers herself 'uninteresting' and thinks that no one will talk to her anyway.

The water is mildly warm and crystal clear, but she does not touch it, watching her mother wash clothes in a large aluminium pan. When hunger overwhelms her, she hangs onto her mother's skirt, whining for food, and then she is given her ration for that day – a banana and small portion of sticky rice. When she begs for an orange, her mother says nothing and goes back to her work with downcast eyes.

One afternoon as she sits alone on the river bank, a shadow falls across the ground in front of the girl, and she suddenly feels a hand resting lightly on her shoulder. Struck with fear, she immediately curls herself up into a small ragged bundle, hiding her face. When she is sure that the stranger has gone away, she turns around cautiously.

One of the small parcels she has seen in other children's hands now lies on the sand directly next to her. Carefully, she tears away the thin brown paper to find a simple picture book with words that she cannot understand. The next time the boat arrives with the woman who hands out parcels, she is waiting for it, her little book locked in her arms. The woman's smile seems kind and assuring, and the girl asks why she comes. The woman laughs and tells her that this is a floating library. The girl does not know what a library is, so she starts to ask questions, which lead to more questions. In the end, her curiosity has been so stimulated that she refuses to go home. Gently, the woman leads her back to her mother.

From that time onwards, the girl looks around continuously, investigating everything that she has missed so far. She throws stones into the water, fascinated by the way the smooth, silken ripples spread towards the shore. She is intensely aware of the warmth of the sun on her face, the rustling of leaves, the texture of the ground under her feet. She rejoices in the sweetness of the fragrant banana which softens in her mouth. She starts to wonder where the river goes to and asks everyone she sees, especially travellers and tradespeople who disembark from the daily boat. When the girl sees a foreign woman for the first time, she is shocked by the colour of her blond hair and white skin. Until then, the girl thought her own hair was light compared to others.

As the girl grows up, her love of books increases. They widen her perspectives and teach her that there is always another world to discover. The Mekong is not just the stretch of water on her doorstep, but a huge river snaking down from the mountains of China through three countries to the sea.

When she is older, she travels down the Mekong to find her first real library. When she visits the huge reclining Buddha in Vientiane, her perspectives change again. The Buddha is so monumental and overwhelming, and life seems so expansive and full of possibilities, that she runs forward to embrace this never-ending adventure.

Questions

Have you lost your sense of curiosity?

Which of your convictions could be seen in a different light?

Which belief about yourself would you like to change?

Is help available from a source you do not want to see?

Are you constantly aware of your immediate physical surroundings and sensations?

What if there were a new joy and a new experience to discover every moment?

As a traveller on life's river, which new destination will you choose?

What if everyone worldwide knew that their beliefs about themselves can be changed at a moment's notice?

What if everyone lived a life of adventure and followed their own personal quest?

"Inner development is the real adventure, the real story, the real biography. True biographies are not written in books. They are written on the paper of the soul. To communicate this story, in words as a writer, or in any way you please, is to be in service to the soul growth of our fellows"

From Seraphin Message 15:
TRUE BIOGRAPHIES ON THE PAPER OF THE SOUL

GLOBAL VILLAGER 41

VITALITY

Global Villager 41 and Shiva as depicted in the painting
THE WORLD–VISION
By Rosie Jackson

GLOBAL VILLAGER 41: VITALITY

Woman aged 38 from Port Louis, Mauritius. Hindu,
lives in poverty and is undernourished, illiterate, has
unsafe drinking water, sexually abused, speaks Hindi

Years of child-bearing and intense caring for her impoverished family has drained this woman of all enthusiasm for life. Chronic tiredness overcomes her at increasingly frequent intervals and she enforces strict control to keep everything going. Often, a severe sore throat forces her to remain absolutely silent. She has to explain to other people that she is ill. At such moments she feels strangled, as if a snake has wrapped itself around her neck and refused to relax its grip. Moving through the day and performing simple household duties turns into slow torture: she is burdened by lethargy, surrounded by complaining children and also by an aggressive, frustrated husband. If he threatens to hit her, she moves faster for a while, but as soon as he is out of sight, she slows down again and sinks into despair.

One evening when her husband returns, he punches his wife in the mouth. The woman washes the blood away, comforts the children and resolves to leave. They are taken in by elderly relatives who have enough room, and who need assistance. They appreciate the woman's help. Seeing that she is in dire need of recuperation, however, they insist that she takes a short break while neighbours look after the children.

In an attempt to reactivate the spiritual side of her life, the woman travels alone to the Hindu festival at the holy lake of Grand Bassin. As the woman looks up at the huge statue of Shiva towering above the forest, she is struck by the power of his gaze. This is Shiva in his capacity as destroyer and transformer. When she sees the snake around his neck, she initially senses the old familiar feeling of constriction around her own neck. At that moment, she knows instinctively that her sore throats are not simply an illness which afflict herself, the victim. They are also a sign of limiting self-expression. Looking at the statue in quiet contemplation, far removed from her daily routine and responsibilities, she sees it change in mood and colour as the light fades and dusk approaches. As night sets in, the woman becomes anxious, but she is so tired that she falls asleep.

At daybreak, she awakes to see the statue in the brilliant morning light. She leaves the fearful shadows of night behind her and feels inwardly uplifted. The snake is no longer a threat but a god of transformation. From then on, the woman learns to express her feelings more and more. Every morning, before continuing with her usual routine, she makes a quick mental plan of how she plans to maintain a high energy level. When she talks to her family and friends, she is aware of every word she uses and tries to convey every fluctuation of feeling. The negative power of words such as 'I am ill' is very clear to her. Instead she offers thanks on a daily basis for her ever-increasing vitality.

Questions

How are you strangling yourself?
How are you strangling others?
How can you increase your self-expression?
What important issue needs to be addressed?
What fear lies behind your feeling of helplessness?
Who would you help next, if helping others were a way of helping yourself?
What morning ritual could provide you with energy and inspiration on a daily basis?
Are you aware of your intrinsic power to create your reality through every thought, word and deed?
What would you like to be able to say about yourself on the day you die?
What if everyone worldwide addressed small problems before they turned into serious problems?

GLOBAL VILLAGER 42: BOUNDLESSNESS

Woman aged 25 from Hong Kong, China. Non-religious, lives in poverty and is undernourished, has unsafe drinking water, literate, speaks Cantonese

The market in the back streets of Hong Kong is crammed with people, and the food stalls have been busy since sunrise. A small woman is squatting on the ground with a knife, about to kill the snake wriggling in front of her. It is destined to become part of the next dish. She is extremely tired, drained by long working hours, but no one seems to be interested in her complaints, or seems to see the dark rings under her eyes. Her only wish is to fall asleep, and sometimes she fantasies about not having to get up any more. When she wakes in the mornings, her memory of the previous long day and the many deadlines which she unflinchingly fulfilled weighs so heavily on her mind that she can hardly pull herself out of bed. In the end, she forces herself to do so at the very last minute and runs out to the market without even having thrown water on her face. She often wonders why everyone is so unfriendly.

One morning, the woman wakes with a start, feeling that something is different. Instead of feeling tired, she is refreshed. To her horror, she realizes that she has overslept. When she arrives at the food stall two hours later than usual, her boss wants to speak with her and she fears the worst. But instead of losing her job as she feared, she is startled to hear that he is very concerned about her. He says that she doesn't need to work such long hours and he shows her how time can be saved here and there by being less particular and more flexible. The woman is more and more astonished and realises that she has great difficulty releasing patterns of behaviour and habits that she has adopted to gain attention or impress others, but which are not essentially necessary and which even create antagonism.

The more she examines her own behaviour, the more she learns to interact with other people in a clear, cheerful and authentic manner. She no longer needs to earn pity and admiration by working long hours. With time, she is so well-versed in methods of reassessing her behaviour and needs, as well as the needs of her workplace, that she is capable of reinventing herself on a daily basis, adjusting immediately and responsibly to all changes in her surroundings. Her major realisation is that she herself has been the most restrictive agent in her life to date, creating her own deadlines. Now she knows that her potential has no bounds, and that she is treading a path which widens into an ever-increasing spiral.

Questions

Do you reinvent yourself on a daily basis?
How many of your 'deadlines' are self-imposed?
Are you leading the sort of life you want to lead?
How often do you reflect upon your own behaviour?
Is it possible to change it?

Is your 'character' a fixed entity or simply a collection of strategies developed to fill a certain need or to reach a certain goal?
Suppose you said the following affirmation daily: "I have no limitations, only ever-increasing potential"?

What if 'tiredness' is something which dominates the lives of people without dreams?
How are you creating your own problems by acting on the need to impress or gain attention?
How does the memory of negative experiences affect your behaviour today?

What if everyone re-examined their behaviour regularly in view of their own needs and also in view of spreading peace and unity worldwide and protecting the resources of our planet?

GLOBAL VILLAGER 43: GRATITUDE

Woman aged 40 from Musan, North Korea. Non-religious,
literate, lives in poverty and is undernourished, speaks Korean

In a small village in the mountains of North Korea near the Chinese border, a woman awakes to find that the water she collected the previous day is covered with ice. Again, winter is on its way and the woman wonders how she will survive it in her small tumbledown cottage together with her three ailing relatives. She stoops when she walks, as if bending under a heavy burden. It is as if she is carrying three old people continuously on her back. They are all ill to varying degrees and all undernourished. Sometimes her son brings them food after finding work at the iron mines in Musan, but at other times they are so hungry that the woman has no other alternative than to collect grass to make into a soup. One day her son brings a newspaper to the village and it is passed from hand to hand with varying degrees of interest. The woman cannot read, but she is astounded by one photograph showing thousands of children in sportswear performing coordinated gymnastics in a large arena. She feels that her life is in stagnation, so far away from city life, and she deeply resents having to care for her relatives. When Chinese businessmen arrive in the village and offer well-paid work in China to the younger, prettier woman who are not yet tied down by family duties, she becomes extremely unhappy and curses her fate.

A few weeks later, on her son's next visit, he finds his mother in a state of deep depression, hardly capable of getting through the day. As usual, he gives her all the news. This time, he has something dreadful to relate. The pretty young women who left the village with the Chinese businessmen were not actually offered jobs after all: they were sold as brides to Chinese farmers on the other side of the border. According to rumour, they lived like slaves in fear of physical violence and had no means of escape.

Although the woman is extremely distraught to hear what has become of her neighbours, she is greatly relieved that she was left behind. But for her elderly relatives, she would have gone too. Gratitude floods through her veins and she experiences a kind of resurrection, regaining her strength and determination. She continues to care lovingly for her elderly relatives who are nearing the end of their lives. The woman finds that she is capable of providing them not only with physical care but also peace of mind. Despite its hardships, life in the mountains so close to nature is now something she would not want to change. She becomes more of a friend to herself, resting when she needs it, and enjoying the company of her neighbours. Often, she practises her own, simple form of meditation, concentrating on the emotion of gratitude and focussing on her heart. The energy flows from her heart into the rest of her body and radiates on her surroundings, causing a spontaneous feeling of content and wellbeing.

Questions

In what way is your crisis self-made?
How often do you express gratitude?
What if you started to write notes in a
'Book of Gratitude' on a daily basis?
What burden can be seen as a blessing?
How could this recognition change your
perception of life and your central role?

When friends disappear, could this be a wake-up call to start being a friend to yourself and others?

Could short but regular periods of quiet contemplation help to clarify your mind?

What is about to end before you have seen its true value?
What if everyone in the world realised that our crises are our own and that others are not to blame?

GLOBAL VILLAGER 44: DISCRETION

Girl aged 16 from Zahedan, Iran. Muslim, lives in poverty, is undernourished, literate, has unsafe drinking water, speaks Baluchi

With shaking hands, a girl picks up the newspaper which her angry father has thrown on the dusty earthen floor. She is being held by local authorities and is under investigation. The photograph on the front page is of herself, together with the announcement of her crime: extremists are demanding that she should be hanged from a crane for immodest conduct; watching football and having sex.

The girl herself, known as an energetic and impetuous friend and daughter in a world where women are forced to learn restraint and patience, has always been defiant. Her monotonous, constricted life in the slums of Zahedan is so unbearable that she slips away at every opportunity for glimpses into another world. In the depths of her soul, she knows that in the end, her behaviour could have dire consequences.

Now she has the proof of it in her hands as she looks at the photograph. Her father is torn between condemning her for being a disgrace to the family and trying to save his beloved daughter.

Finally, the man decides to take action and approaches foreign tourists coming out of a hotel in one of the better areas of Zahedan. He cannot make himself understood, but he gives them the newspaper. From the desperation in his voice, they sense his great fear and promise to find out what the newspaper says.

The travellers, in turn, are shocked to hear about the girl's proposed punishment and they contact international human rights groups which exert pressure on the authorities, demanding her release.

When she is allowed to return home, her father tells her how it came about, and she starts to see him in a completely different light. Now he is more of a caring individual rather than an implacable, authoritarian figure.

Having come so close to execution, she is impelled to investigate near death experiences. She learns that life is eternal, and that death is merely a transformation – a re-entry into light and communion with the universe. She knows that the timing of her arrest was perfect timing for her soul's agenda and that it was also a catalyst for something new.

From then on, she also tries to emulate her father's discretion when dealing with personal matters among family and friends, recognizing that her behaviour has often been insensitive in the past. Her increasing self-respect makes defiance unnecessary and instead, she approaches others with love. She learns to wait and think before she blurts out some derogatory comment. She dreams about swimming with dolphins, approaching them slowly and carefully.

As the girl becomes more sensitive to the needs and feelings of others, the world around her also becomes more sensitised. As the world moves ever onwards into a higher spiritual vibration, as a result of the high-quality behaviour of this girl and of all global citizens, the death penalty is abolished in all countries. The absurdity of killing someone to show that it is wrong to kill someone else has been recognised, and this becomes part of public awareness worldwide.

Just like the high frequencies which abound in the communication of dolphins, sexuality is seen as the ultimate expression of spiritual love – a way of heightening the intensity of compassion and joy on the planet.

Questions

What do you continue doing although you are aware of extreme consequences?

What has 'died' to help you to gain new perspectives and new experiences?

Does something have to end in a radical way so that you come to a certain realisation?

How much of your behaviour is not a chosen path but a reaction to convention?

Do you feel betrayed by your sex?

Could your view of the opposite sex be stereotyped?

Do you burst out with bitter comments which are the result of unhealed internal wounds?

How can you intensify your experience of compassion and joy? What needs to heal so that you can release defiant attitudes and approach others with love and sensitivity?

What if everyone knew that death is simply a transition, a re-entry into light?

GLOBAL VILLAGER 44
DISCRETION

Global Villager 44 and the dolphins as depicted in
THE WORLD-VISION
A painting by Rosie Jackson

GLOBAL VILLAGER 45: HUMILITY

Woman aged 32 from Galle, Sri Lanka. Buddhist, lives in poverty and is undernourished, literate, has unsafe drinking water, is pregnant, speaks Singhalese

A dejected woman stands in a long queue in front of a makeshift soup kitchen. She is one of a million displaced people following devastation caused by a large tsunami along Sri Lanka's coastline. She feels completely lethargic, traumatized by the death of her mother and the wreckage of the home she so proudly built from her savings. It also demolished the hotel where she worked as a batik artist. Her husband's taxi lies like a corpse on the beach and his driving license is floating somewhere in the sea.

When she sees the waves, still coughing human bones onto the shore, she averts her terrified gaze and walks towards the food kitchen with her plate to stand in line with the others. She recognizes some of them – neighbours she used to look down on for lounging around and being out of work. She cannot bear being reduced to their level and being robbed of all her possessions.

All her family's belongings are now contained in one small box which she keeps in her hands. Her husband is helping destitute elderly relatives in another part of the country. She is pregnant, and she wonders how she will be able to manage on her own when her baby is born.

After initial failure to get through, donations from abroad start to trickle into the area and are distributed by dedicated local doctors and helpers. When the woman is offered a roof over her head, a mattress and new cooking utensils, her cheeks burn with shame. For one second, pride engulfs her like a tornado, but in the next it dissipates, leaving her with the strange feeling of being completely hollow. The woman humbly accepts the assistance offered and expresses her unending gratitude.

Later, no longer provided for by the camp, she is forced to rely on her own initiative. She shares what little she has with her neighbours who support her in return, especially when the baby comes. Her behaviour as a mother becomes purely instinctive. Her instant response to her crying child shows that she has learnt to act from the heart before she thinks, and her demonstration of love and humility is an inspiration to those who find difficulty re-assessing their values when confronted by material loss.

Questions

What trauma has occurred, enabling you to give birth to something new?

How much weight do you give material possessions in your life?

Who deserves more of your respect?

Which situation is inviting you to show the quality of humility?

Is it possible that losing something is a way of finding your lost self?

In what way have you cut yourself off from your instincts?

How quickly do 'second thoughts' interrupt your flow of intuitive action and encourage 'separateness' from others?

What if everyone believed the more we give, the more we receive?

If everyone were as special as everyone else, how would we treat each other and what would stop us from starting a golden age of peace on earth?

GLOBAL VILLAGER 46: RESPONSIBILITY

Woman aged 23 from Bangkok, Thailand. Non-religious, smokes, literate, sexually abused, speaks Thai

A petite naked woman sits on the lap of a huge, red-skinned European who has just selected her from a line-up of thirty available prostitutes. They have just arrived on the island of Ko Samat, stepping down from the boat into shallow turquoise waves, to rent a hut on the idyllic beaches. Whenever she has sex with him, she feels guilty, but she doesn't say why. She suspects that she has AIDS, but she turns a blind eye and doesn't get herself tested. This fear lurks in her subconscious and shakes her inner serenity. Every step seems more uncertain with every man she accompanies through the wet sand to the beaches. And back in Bangkok after every excursion, her sense of security is weakened by the sight of locals protesting in the streets against power and corruption. When an incurable sore appears on her thigh, she sticks a plaster over it rather than asking herself the cause.

When the next customer prefers to stay with her in Bangkok to see the sights, instead of lying on the beach, her insecurity grows even more. While visiting Bangkok's golden palace, she is extremely disturbed by the Wat Phra Kaew guard figures with their grim facial expressions and the way they support the walls. At the sight of a statue which is half woman and half lion, she bursts into uncontrollable sobs. The customer comforts her and she finds herself telling him about her fears, her inner conflicts, her poverty-stricken family whom she is trying to support and her inability to follow her own intuition.

The man, who is basically good-natured, is appalled and tries to help her. Instead of seeing her as a pleasant passing companion he understands that she is a woman of great depth and potential. He treasures her honesty and is fascinated by her increasing willingness to open up. At first, she feels exposed and vulnerable when she shows her feelings, but she sees that honesty increases intimacy and trust. She even confides her mother's darkest secret which has instilled her with a fear of death for as long as she can remember: her mother worked for the postal service, regularly labelling and sending small parcels to the USA. Years later, she discovered that these were the remains of American soldiers who died in Vietnam. The woman now faces her fear of death and decides that she will test herself for AIDS, taking on full responsibility for herself. She never forgets the statue which precipitated her great change. Now, her "active" nature and her "intuitive" nature are in harmonious balance.

Questions

Are you turning a 'blind eye'?
Can this endanger others?
How does your consideration for others prevent you
from looking after yourself?
How are you inwardly shaken, and how long will you
wait before you speak openly?
In what way are you consciously 'selling' or
disempowering yourself?
What choice has always been there,
but which you have failed to see?

Are the two sides of yourself – the fluid, intuitive 'female' side
and the active, energetic 'lion' or 'male' side – in harmony with
each other or out of balance?

Does 'security' exist? Could 'insecurity' simply be a lack of
understanding that life is a series of ever changing-cycles
which we ourselves instigate to fulfil our potential?

What if everyone showed their feelings all the time with the
purpose of building a network of honesty, trust and intimacy
around the world?

GLOBAL VILLAGER 47: REVERENCE

Woman aged 64 from Hiroshima, Japan. Buddhist, literate, overweight, has diabetes, sexually abused, speaks Japanese

A woman stands absent-mindedly in a garden, regretting her decision to move away from the city. She is wearing the traditional dress which is expected of her on certain occasions. Although she has never actually told anyone, she dislikes wearing it. Sometimes she wonders if her female friends feel the same, but she is not on particularly close terms with them, and wouldn't dream of asking. The woman also dislikes looking after her large property which she inherited unexpectedly from a distant aunt who she had never known. Pruning bushes, weeding the flower beds and mowing the lawn has turned into a never-ending, pointless exercise. However, she forces herself to do what is expected of her and keeps the garden under the sort of control which she exerts over all other aspects of her life.

Following a long visit to her family in the city, and following an extensive period of rain, the woman returns find the garden in an exuberant state of rampant growth. She is filled with a feeling of utter despair in the knowledge that weeds will always grow. Wondering why her aunt wanted to live in such a huge, isolated house with its extensive grounds, she sorts through some old letters. These reveal an old family secret: her aunt was badly mutilated by the Hiroshima atom bomb and forced to live hidden from the public eye. The garden was her greatest solace.

The woman's attitude changes rapidly. Weeds are no longer weeds but miracles of survival, especially in an area affected by the atom bomb. Nature teaches her certain cosmic rules – that we reap what we sow, and that a seed will die if it stops growing. She greets the seeds, sun and water as living beings, recognising their divinity. If she intends to prune a tree, she gives prior warning so that tree has time to pull away its energy, thus avoiding pain. In the name of every human being, she thanks the earth every morning for her presence and generosity, without which humankind could not continue living. Showered with love, respect and perfect conditions, her plants grow prolifically and produce spectacular and unusual flowers. The woman no longer wears her traditional Kimono. Instead her dresses are flowing and her hair entwined with leaves and flowers. She merges with nature as part of the eternal cycle.

Questions

How conscious are you of the miracle of growth?
Which part of yourself are you hiding from the 'public eye'?
What has hurt you so much that you are afraid of losing control?
Do you cut off new opportunities or avenues rather than waiting to see how things grow and develop?
What do you curb or kill in order to retain control and fend off fear?
What would you do next if traditional roles and conventional attitudes disappeared overnight?
What if everyone was encouraged to grow naturally in the direction which fascinated them most?
To what extent do you do what is expected of you?
Could you be on better terms with your 'sisters' or 'brothers'?
Do you focus more on the weeds in life's garden,
or more on the abundance or colour in life's garden?
Are you aware that your experiences are the result of seeds you have sown?
Is it possible for you to withdraw energy from 'branches' which no longer serve you or others?

What if everyone saw the divine in every living cell,
considered themselves part of every living cell
and respected the life in every living cell?

GLOBAL VILLAGER 48: CREATIVITY

Man aged 22 from Tokyo, Japan. Non-religious, literate, smokes, drinks, speaks Japanese

A thin young man is sitting at a table covered in debris. Stale smelling cigarette ash and left-over noodles from two days ago have not been cleared away. His shoulders are hunched, and his face is pale and anxious when he sees that his packet of cigarettes is nearly empty. Holding the last one in his slender fingers, he runs his other hand through his dyed brown hair.

Plagued by headaches and worried about cancer and AIDS, he wonders why his partner has started coming home late, but so far, he has not had the courage to ask. Slumping onto the sofa, he crushes some sheets of paper on which he has jotted a few notes, his sensitive observations on the feelings of people and animals around him. He could probably be a short story writer if he did not feel so numbed by self-doubt and fear.

As a homosexual (and these do not officially exist in his country), he often harbours a strange conviction that he might actually be invisible. All men tend to be married, irrespective of their sexual tendencies. As he picks up the newspaper, his heart contracts when he sees a photograph of oil-covered birds in Hokkaido. Like them, he feels incapacitated and forlorn. He regards his fear as a sane reaction to deal with a confusing, inhospitable world.

When his partner fails to return home, the young man's fear runs so deep that he decides the time has come for action. In the midst of his pain, it occurs to him that his fear may actually be the cause and not the result of his situation. He decides to put this to the test, giving his fear full reign. He visualises his partner in the neighbourhood bar, talking intimately to someone else. Then he goes to the bar and opens the door very slowly. As he looks fearfully into the room he sees exactly the situation he has visualised.

At first, he is shocked by this discovery, but then he realises that the opposite must also be true; if he is absolutely confident that something positive will happen, then it will. As a result of this realisation, he is overwhelmed with joy, gratitude, and the knowledge that he can create his own destiny. He follows his heart and writes articles and letters in support of the Hokkaido birds, committing to himself and to others in need. Writing turns into his unique way of communicating to others the creative process of life.

Questions

How can you increase your creativity?
How open are you about your sexual leanings?
Is there any situation in which you feel invisible?

What if headaches are not simply a result of stress, over-drinking or insufficient sleep, but a message in your subconscious which is trying to get out and be heard?

What fear, if you dig deeply enough, is responsible for your negative experiences?

What if enthusiasm, joy and self-confidence are responsible for your positive experiences?

Are you aware that visualisation is the first step towards manifestation?

What if everybody worldwide realised that their thoughts and feelings were precursors of the future events in their lives?

What if everyone realised that the quality of their thoughts determined the quality of their experience?

GLOBAL VILLAGER 49: REVALUATION

Girl aged 19 from Ulan Bator, Mongolia
Non-religious, literate, speaks Mongolian

Folding her arms, a young woman listens to a group of girls comforting a friend who has got pregnant by mistake. The young woman smiles disdainfully. She is sure that she would never be so foolish. She stands proudly on a paved square in Ulan Bator, in the shadow of a huge statue of a soldier parading a socialist flag. As a student, she is very critical of all old structures, and she is very sensitive to the criticism of elderly people.

Similarly, she is spontaneous and enthusiastic about all things new, and every time she passes the statue on the square, the sight of the young, fearless soldier floods her with a surge of energy. She is happy to be living in Ulan Bator – the only place in Mongolia where anything happens – despite the monotone concrete blocks and smog. On the contrary, she is impressed by the number, size and grandeur of these buildings compared with the one-roomed yurt she grew up in on the deserted Mongolian plains. She is happiest being seen in enormous discos, or translating for foreigners who disembark from the train in Ulan Bator during the summer months. She is unhappiest when she finds herself alone or arguing with her companions, and she does not understand why this happens so often.

When she walks home after the disco one evening, she steps into the road without looking, causing a man on a bicycle to swerve. He shouts at her, and she flares up immediately, shouting insults. The man goes up to her, grabs her roughly by the shoulders and threatens to rape her. The girl suddenly remembers the scene on the square where she scornfully watched the pregnant girl. In that instant, she understands that she has to change her lack of respect, and she apologises to the injured man. He apologises too, saying that he has had a terrible day and is sorry for suddenly taking it out on her.

The whole incident shakes her to the core, and she suddenly feels a strong desire to revisit her home on the deserted Mongolian plains. As she used to do in her childhood, she walks round a shrine of branches hung with blue material. After three ceremonial circumlocutions, she makes an offering of a blue scarf to encourage good grazing grounds for her family's livestock. Slowly, her view of her home changes. Instead of seeing 'nothing' in this wide expanse of land, she sees huge unfenced vistas and wide-open skies which fill her with a sense of eternity and release. When she sees kids and lambs inside the family yurt, memories of her delight as a child are reawakened and she relives her own innocent joy. As she readjusts to the slower pace of nomadic life, she learns to wait and reflect more before verbalising criticism or jumping to defend her ego. She reassesses her view of her nomad past, appreciating her roots as a necessary base from which she has been able to develop exactly those qualities and experiences which lie on her soul's agenda.

Questions

Are you over-critical?
What if you learned to wait more?
Have you the right to judge other people?
How much does your ego control your behaviour?
How often do you jump to defend yourself immediately?
What if another person's anger has very little to do with you?
Which fences have you built which separate you from others?
What if your view of others is biased by your own experience?
What if your own anger has nothing to do with anyone else?
What have you sacrificed in pursuit of excitement and action?
What new, fast avenue are you pursuing, blinding you to forgotten resources from the past?

GLOBAL VILLAGER 50: TENACITY

Baby boy aged 7 months from Kashmir, Pakistan
Muslim, lives in poverty and is undernourished

Sitting on his mother's knee, the small baby instinctively reaches for his mother's breast. She has been carrying him on her back for most of the day, desperate to get as far away as possible from the earthquake zone where she has lost everything. On the one hand, the baby is reassured by the close physical proximity to his mother, but he also senses the continuous tension in her body which is born of fear.

When she walks, he is unsettled by her jerky movements, by the limp resulting from her leg injury, and his weak, forlorn cries go largely unnoticed. When they stop to breastfeed, there is very little milk and he is plagued by hunger, but in the end he decides it is not worth screaming for something which is not there.

After three days of life on the road, the baby has reached its limit. Instead of resigning himself to the lack of milk, the baby starts to scream endlessly. Despite his mother's attempts to soothe him, the baby does not give up. He screams so loudly that his mother stops walking. It is only now that she realises that her foot is actually injured, and she collapses in pain.

When the next person passes, she implores him to tell her where she can find medical help. He takes pity on her and brings her to the nearest medical centre for treatment. The baby is given extra food and is glad to be off the road and in caring hands.

As time passes, his mother improves in health and can give him the milk he has fought for. He has learnt not to give up. Soon he can run after the butterflies which so fascinate him. The knowledge that perseverance leads to success continues to motivate him in all spheres of life – not only as a toddler learning to walk, but as a child learning to write, and as a man following his own path. He is rarely afflicted by feelings of resignation as an adult. Whenever such feelings do arise, he acknowledges them as vestiges of his childhood experiences during the earthquake and is able to move forward with confidence and vigour, drawing a definite line between the past and the present.

Questions

When did you last scream?
What role does resignation play in your life?
What if everyone worldwide took their own needs seriously?

Have you stopped asking for something because you think it is not there?

How often do you say:
"There's nothing I can do" or
"That's the way life is"?

What tumultuous event in early childhood still affects your behaviour today?

How many decisions affecting your life are made by other people?

Supposing you make all decisions, including the decision not to make one?

What will you say if you find your own 'voice' again and make it heard?

Which pattern of behaviour was appropriate as a child but is no longer appropriate in your life as an adult?

GLOBAL VILLAGER 51: SENSUALITY

Woman aged 27 from Kashmir, Pakistan
Muslim, illiterate, speaks Kashmiri

A limping woman rests momentarily at the roadside, carrying nothing but her child and a few personal possessions. Her eyes are wild with fear as she relives the events of the past days. She recalls her overwhelming panic as she felt the ground shake and heard the earth roar. The moment she ran out of the house with her baby, the simple structure crumbled – like a film in slow motion – and fell into a deep crevasse. The shock has taken its toll on her body, and the baby cries feebly because she has so little milk. In her prolonged searches for water, she tries to ignore the pain in her foot and the scenes of devastation she encounters. Clenching her meagre belongings, she walks on to find her relatives in a distant town. She imagines being confronted by a gang of men who abduct her baby and distort its limbs so that it turns into a beggar child who can earn them money. She clutches the child firmly to her breast, aware of her insecure position as a woman alone, seeing potential kidnappers in every passer-by. The child whimpers, sensing her constant fear.

After three days on the road, the baby screams so bitterly and continuously that it pierces her heart and she finds that she cannot bring herself to continue. When the next person passes, she appeals to him to tell her where the nearest medical care can be found. Once she has admitted her pain, her leg throbs unbearably and she is unable to ignore it. The man takes pity on her and organises transport to a local hospital. The doctor tells her that the foot is not only strained but broken. He does not understand how she could have walked so far. The doctor forbids her to move and recommends a daily spoonful of apricot oil to strengthen the baby.

The doctor tells her about his own childhood in the narrow, isolated Hunza valley – about his simple diet of potatoes and fresh
apricots, the fasting and dancing throughout the winter months,
the festivities when all couples married on December 21st, the
complete absence of worry, the knowledge that everyone was
your sister or brother, the burning sun, the invigorating coldness
and clarity of the mountain air at high altitude. Soon the woman
can breastfeed her baby again, and as she does so, she falls into
pleasant reveries, imagining a life of plenty with a never-ending
supply of succulent apricots. She sees herself completely empowered, dancing in a paradise with her face towards the sun,
fully aware of every sensual sensation in her body. The more she
visualizes a life in which celebrating love and expressing joy is
not confined to family or home situations, the more she draws
this experience into her own life and into the lives of others so
that it spreads to all those around her. For them, every day is a
wedding day.

Questions

Are you on the edge of an abyss?
How much do you respect yourself?
How often do you imagine the worst?
How far do you go before you notice pain?
What fear impels you to overstep your limit?
Is there any way you could respect others more?
Could you enjoy the sensual side of life more fully?

What if by expecting something good, it actually happens?

What if every person worldwide regarded 'natural disasters'
as a reminder of the necessity for radical change in their
personal behaviour?

Can you imagine a world where everyone celebrates every day
like a wedding day?

GLOBAL VILLAGER 52:
JOY OF EXPERIMENTATION

Boy aged 12 from Pura Besaki, Bali
Hindu, literate, speaks Balinese

The temples on the ancient mountain site of Pura Besakih are decorated with flowers. Women wander by, carrying baskets on their heads containing food and offerings for the gods. A twelve-year-old boy stands watching them, feeling a little forlorn. He remembers the shoulder yoke which his parents have given him so that he can help them with work in the fields. Soon he will have to carry loads too. The boy does not feel very special, although it is a special ceremonial day. The traditional cleansing rituals which fill others with a sense of peaceful elation, have surprisingly little effect on him. Despite the serenity of the temples, he cannot forget the disturbing noises – women quarrelling, horns blowing, hawkers, tourists or hens squawking – which accompany him throughout the day. He was treated like a god for the first year of his life, allowed to do whatever he liked, but now he is in limbo somewhere between childhood and manhood. The boy is caught up in expectations and strong family ties, conflicting with his own needs and desire to experiment. The boy is confused about his position, and despite his agility and light-footedness he is burdened by a sense of heaviness. His parents subsist on very little. How will he be able to support himself in the future? There seems to be no time to play anymore.

As he stands there waiting at the temple, his mother suddenly appears and sees that he is sad. "Why aren't you playing?" she enquires, and carries flowers into the temple. The boy is just about to join the other children when his father appears and admonishes him. "Why aren't you working and helping your mother?" The boy stops dead in his tracks. The bubble of pressure bursts inside him. Screaming, he falls to the ground in a state of shock and faints. When he comes around, he is back home with both parents at this bedside. With their encourage-ment, he is able to tell them his feelings of great confusion. Both of them tell him gently that it is a time of great change. From now on, he will start to make his own decisions and define his own path. 'Play' is not something which he has left behind him but something he can integrate into his voyage of discovery. He can play, experiment and be creative in all aspects of life.

His parents give him a present to symbolize this – a set of simple juggling balls. The boy is greatly relieved and starts to juggle whenever he feels the old worries resurfacing, rejoicing in the flow of movement. He looks forward to the chances he will create in his own life and the way he will move on from one game to the next, irrespective of whether he 'wins' or 'loses'. He develops his own rituals on a regular basis, while still respecting the traditional rituals which take place at the myriad temples of Pura Besakih. Fully aware that his home lies at the foot of an active volcano, he takes things lightly, knowing that it could erupt at any time. By the time he is a man, he has an unshaken belief in his own self-worth and knows that he has a divine path to follow.

Questions

Whose opinion counts?
How can you relax deeply on a daily basis?
Are you following your divine path, or do you deviate?
We all have 'time', so how do you choose to spend it?
To what extent has 'enjoying yourself" been suppressed?
Will you take time today to have a wonderful experience?
How often do you experiment with new structures in your life?

How often do you feel you are compromising yourself in order to fit in with the picture that other people have of you?

What if everyone worldwide rejoiced in experimentation and discovery at all levels?

GLOBAL VILLAGER 53: DEVOTION

Man aged 30 from Phnom Penn, Cambodia. Buddhist, lives in poverty and is undernourished, literate, speaks Khmer

A faded blue hat falls over the eyes of a motorbike-taxi driver. He slumps exhausted into the shady seat where so many of his customers have sat before him. His cut-off gloves, which protect his hands from the sun while driving, lie on the seat beside him. His dirty white shirt, the only one he owns, is drenched with sweat. His day's work is over, and while he has ferried a considerable number of customers across town, he is still worried about tomorrow. Every morning he wakes up wondering whether he can afford to pay for fuel, which is getting more expensive by the day.

Sometimes he wishes that his faith in Buddhism was stronger. While he is familiar with all the rituals his mother has taught him, they do not seem to have any meaning for him as he struggles to survive in the crazy traffic and polluted streets. Whenever his route forces him to pass the former interrogation prison of the Khmer Rouge, where a member of his family died, he feels even more helpless. He feels that he is a victim of forces greater than himself. In an attempt to forget this, and to forget his three hungry daughters who are waiting for him, he often spends a portion of his wages on drink. When he arrives home drunk, his wife is bound to shout at him, and he is bound to hit her.

One evening the man returns so drunk and abuses his wife so much that she collapses on the floor bleeding, surrounded by their three crying daughters. Shocked, he recovers his senses, trying in vain to find a doctor. Eventually, he finds a makeshift hospital where she can be treated. Meanwhile he is unable to take to the streets in his taxi because he has to look after his small girls. He begs their forgiveness for his violence. Gradually, the children become less reticent, opening their hearts more and more when they see how devotedly he cares for them. They see that he is increasingly motivated by love. Eventually, their mother recovers and the family is reconciled. For the first time, the man's focus is not purely on his work, though his working day is much the same. The man registers the small miracles which surround him: the smiles of his daughters, the tiny flowers which always open at ten in the morning and close at midday. He enjoys the smells of the food stalls he passes, the bright colours of piled fruit, patches of dancing light falling through the trees, and the tall buildings which cast long shadows on shady streets. He greets everyone who approaches him with the desire to help them in any way he can. His ready enthusiasm is appreciated by his customers and soon he is employed by several people on a regular basis. As his work in the community grows, he enters politics and begins to represent the local people, giving interviews in newspapers and looking for new ways to achieve equality for all. However, he also sees politics as an expression of spirituality. Principally, he teaches the lesson of his own experience: that the more devotion you show, the more you receive.

Questions

Are you a victim?
How are you abusing your own body?
Are you aware that you produce your own crises?
What if worrying is just a projection into the future?
What strategies have you developed to hide your sadness?
Are you in danger of hurting another through your frustration?
How much longer do you plan to wait before changing a
damaging habit which could have serious consequences?
What if your sadness can be eradicated by relieving the
sadness of someone else?
How would the world change if everyone gave what they
wanted to receive?
How aware are you of the 'Boomerang' principle – that all
energy you send out (negative and positive) returns to you
as a physical experience?

GLOBAL VILLAGER 54: LIGHT HEARTEDNESS

Man aged 51 from Burma. Christian, lives in poverty,
is undernourished, illiterate, speaks Karen

A rickety suspension bridge made of wooden planks and rope swings high above an isolated ravine in the Burmese jungle. A man stands at one end of the bridge, wondering whether to cross it. This is the first time he has ventured so far in ten years. Although one part of him wants to rush across the bridge to the other side, throwing off the intense feelings of fear which have burdened him for so long, his right side seems to be paralysed. As he stands on the precarious rocks above the gorge, he remembers the years he has spent living in hiding as members of a persecuted tribe in the Burmese hills. Without him, the elder members of his family would not have survived. But now his parents are dead. Although his friends urge him to leave the past behind, the man cannot move forward when he thinks of their pain and how they filled his life with suffocating closeness.

As he looks up to the other end of the bridge, he sees someone coming towards him. He immediately runs for cover, his heart pounding. As always, his first instinct is to hide, but as the person approaches, it is just a harmless young boy carrying something on his back. The man realizes that fear dictates his every move; he decides to summon all his courage and cross the bridge.

For him, it is like entering another world. The man reaches a small village, renews acquaintances and catches up with developments and events, and he realises that it was not absolutely necessary for him to stay in continuous hiding for such long, consecutive periods. Even in dangerous circumstances, he would have had connections or places to stay, run by people 'underground'. He knows now that his great fear and lack of knowledge led him to choose to stay there on a constant basis, looking after his ill parents and family. He sees that he was comparatively 'free' all the time, and that he in effect imprisoned himself.

While he is still on comparatively dangerous ground, he has a wider perspective and is able to regard his previous dilemma in a completely different light. His tribe calls their land 'Kwathodei', meaning 'land of light'. The man realises the significance of this for his own experience: we are always living in a land of light if we look beyond the shadows.

Questions

What is suffocating you?
Which bridge are you afraid to cross?
What fear lies behind your rejection of freedom?
Do you have a choice in the way you see things?

What if you took responsibility for yourself as seriously as you take your responsibility for others?

If you view the future as a blank page, where nothing is predetermined, which steps will you take next?

Is it possible that you are only aware of certain 'jigsaw pieces' in your life?

If you gained a wider perspective, how could you regard the complete picture in a different light?

What if everyone introduced a more light-hearted approach to their problems?

What would happen if everyone knew that they lived in a land of light?

GLOBAL VILLAGER 55: FAIRNESS

Man aged 56 from Abu Dhabi, United Arab Emirates
Muslim, rich, literate, overweight, smokes, speaks Arabic

A large parcel has arrived for a wealthy businessman whose office is situated at the very top of a tall, white skyscraper. Among other things, the parcel contains the newest and best mobile phone available. The man hopes it will help him save time.

Though he earns very well, and though his every physical need is satisfied, he sometimes has the feeling that he is in prison, far away from all his acquaintances, losing touch with them and with himself. Sometimes he is overcome by a fear of illness, and he has an irrepressible desire to hide, but this is very difficult as he is head of a large family. Instead of driving home after work to the guarded compound around his luxurious house, he often plays dominoes in the company of other men, and spends the night at a hotel.

On business trips, he is relieved to be somewhere else, but he sometimes finds himself in insalubrious places or countries. He walks as quickly as possible through dirt-ridden streets in his white robes. He also feels that he is treated like dirt. He is happy to return to sparkling clean offices, but simultaneously he feels the strong absence of deeper meaning in his life and feels somehow impure.

During a business trip to Pakistan, a passing woman knocks into him by mistake on the streets. The man is so enraged that he shouts and curses, but he cannot pursue her because an agonizing pain streaks though his body and he falls to the ground. Later, he is diagnosed with a serious disease. This major confirmation of his fears impels him to investigate the connection between outer circumstances and his inner state of being. He realizes that wherever he is, his surroundings mirror his 'polluted' mind and lack of respect, especially towards women. He is now very conscious of the fact that every puff of his cigarette is a step closer to his physical demise, and he realizes that he does not love himself. In addition to regular physical checks he engages in regular meditation and focusses on cleansing his mental and emotional bodies. He spends more time with his family and also with his new falcon, slowly building stable and loving relationships. In the course of his travels, he comes across the African saying: "Every man is a different country", which impels him to respect everyone, irrespective of sex, rank and race. He becomes increasingly prominent, standing up for the rights of 'minorities' which he now realises is his life's fulfilment. As a result, he himself is held in high esteem and treated with great respect.

Questions

Who could you treat more fairly?

Have you lost sight of your life's purpose?

What lies behind your harshness to yourself?

What if you honoured and respected everyone?

What fear lies behind the desire to be somewhere else?

What do you feel inwardly that you do not show outwardly?

What if everyone worldwide acted fairly and decided not to participate in any form of sexual harassment or make any more derogatory comments about women or men?

How would the world change if everyone meditated regularly in order to cleanse themselves emotionally and mentally?

GLOBAL VILLAGER 56: CONCENTRATION

Man aged 77 from Nepal. Buddhist, will soon die, lives in
poverty and is undernourished, illiterate, speaks Nepalese

An elderly man is sitting in a cramped mountain shrine in the
Himalayas in Nepal, but he is distracted. Apart from the screams
of small children running around outside, he is preoccupied with
angry thoughts about the wide, new road which is being built
through his valley. He suspects that the road serves dubious political purposes, or perhaps it is preparing the way for even more
tourists. Physically, the man's health is not good, and he knows
that he has not much time left in this world. He shudders at the
cockroach crawling at his feet, which suggests to him that death
is close at hand.

The cockroach disturbs him so much that he decides to break off
his meditation and go out into the mountains. On a sudden whim,
he turns down a path he has never taken before, although he has
often passed this way. As he climbs slowly up the hillside, he
suddenly sees a pink, bell-shaped flower. Giving thanks, he picks
it and carries it back in his gnarled hand. He has found a nard –
a holy plant which has the ability to open the heart and clear
doubts.

From then on, cockroaches do not enter the shrine when the man
meditates, because the man's energy level is so high and his
spiritual connection to the Divine so strong. When a child giggles
and shouts, he merely smiles. Despite his nearness to death, he
travels to the stupas of Swayamhunath, one of the holiest places
in the Kathmandu valley, renowned for its mystical light in early
morning. He sits there in quiet serenity, surrounded by white
shrines, orange prayer flags and pilgrims who tell him inspiring
stories about rainbow consciousness. He knows it is time to slow
down and honour himself. His journey is about to continue elsewhere, and the essence of that journey is that it never ends.

Questions

Is it time to slow down?

How often do you follow a sudden whim?

Are you fully aware that you create your own experience?

Which self-imposed or accepted rules govern your journey?

How can you become more centred and more concentrated?

Is it time to take a path which has always been there,
but which you have never considered before?

How easily do you come to terms with change,
which is the only thing we can rely on?

What would change if meditation formed a regular part of
your daily routine?

What if the quality of your thoughts formed the richness of
your experience?

Supposing everyone managed to retain inner balance all the
time, irrespective of outward circumstances?

GLOBAL VILLAGER 57: DECISIVENESS

Man aged 30 from Sumatra, Indonesia. Muslim, lives in poverty and is undernourished, literate, speaks Minangkabau

A man stares out over the river, watching the trees - which he has just felled - floating down the river. He has been told that when they reach their destination they will be used for making benches, but he cannot be entirely sure as he never travels far from his home. He earns enough to keep himself and his family, but feels uneasy because he is actually cutting down his own hunting grounds, and reduced hunting grounds was his reason for turning to logging in the first place. At night, his sleep is fitful and he has frightening dreams which leave him with a feeling of exhaustion in the mornings. Subconsciously, he knows he is part of a vicious circle of self-destruction and that he is ignoring his natural protective instinct for the earth.

When he wakes one morning, the river sounds louder than usual and the man rushes out of his small hut to see what is happening. The river is nearly flooding its banks, and the water has turned to chocolate brown. He bends down and runs his fingers through it, only to find that it has acquired the consistency of soft mud. When the water returns to its normal colour, he dismisses the phenomenon as the result of heavy rains upstream. But the next day it happens again. Wondering whether the mud will kill the fish he catches and eats, the man feels a strange tightening in his stomach and starts to worry about the river. He decides to follow his hunch that the increasing floods have an unnatural cause and he travels upstream to investigate.

To his horror, he discovers large areas of widespread deforestation, and to his horror he learns that his forest is being decimated to make toilet rolls and newspapers. Knowing that his survival depends on it, the man goes into action, informing all the villages down river and contacting newspapers. He realizes that he has avoided taking on responsibility. Knowing that his survival depends upon it, he becomes increasingly decisive and sets his priorities which are long-term and global. The faster he makes decisions, the quicker things happen. Through the protests staged by the villagers, the logging process is forced to slow down. Not only is the river flowing again as it should, but his own life is also in flow.

As discussions on the future of the forest continue, the man's dedication is so great that he is seen as a champion of fragile ecologies. As he walks through the forest, he embraces each new tree which sprouts miraculously from the trunks of trees already felled. His investigations lead to him to new methods of protecting the earth and the water which is her life's blood. He envisages polluted rivers being cleansed by enormous crystals, and he envisages new, unusual birds coming to roost in the regenerated forests. His decisions are governed by his overwhelming love for the planet.

Questions

How much do you respect yourself?
In what way are you destroying yourself?
What unpleasant circumstances do you ignore?
What would change if you were more decisive?
Are you in a vicious circle, and what part do you play in it?
Can you accept that everything is an expression of Divinity?

What if you focussed on long-term fulfilment,
instead of short-term fixes?

If you fully understood that you are capable of great things, what will you do next?

What if everyone considered the protection of the environment in every decision they made?

GLOBAL VILLAGER 58: CONTEMPLATION

Woman aged 47 from Banda Aceh, Indonesia.
Muslim, literate, speaks Aceh

The ocean seems quite calm as the woman looks out to sea, but she is overwhelmed by horrific memories of the recent tsunami which killed sixty thousand people in Banda Aceh. She stretches her arms into the air, begging for mercy, praying that it will never happen again. Often, she cannot move, rooted to the spot by grief. During the day, she stares out at the sea, and during the night she dreams of corpses and woks stuck in swamps of black mud. She finds it extremely difficult to move on, in both the physical and mental sense. While she has not actually lost any members of her family because they all managed to take refuge in the mosque, she has lost a number of old friends who have borne witness to her life over many years. A leg injury she suffered during the tsunami means that she cannot walk fast, or help, or move much in any direction. This is a distressing limitation for her, as she is known as an extremely energetic, hard-working woman.

One day, the woman's leg feels so stiff that she is unable to go to the seashore as usual. She is seized with a terrible feeling of emptiness. She realizes that she is somehow addicted to mourning her losses on a daily basis. At home, surrounded by her family, she is forced to watch progress, instead of focusing on the past. Many signs of devastation have been combatted, and some sort of order has been re-established. The children go to a school which has been set up in a tent, and houses are being rebuilt. The woman has to accept that she too is one of the "wounded", and she is grateful for the help of her family. In this situation, she learns that it is all right to slow down, if her body needs it.

Turning from outer horrors to long stretches of inner contemplation, she gradually comes to the conclusion that she was already 'wounded' before the tsunami. The very demanding pace she set herself previous to the disaster was actually already causing pain in her leg. She recognises that her body is a messenger and that it has sent her a very pertinent warning to 'go slow' before it is too late. Now is the time for inner reflection. Recognising her neglect of herself on all levels, and admitting her inner stagnation, she decides to make her mental and spiritual health a priority. In her undaunted, constant activity previous to the tsunami, she often scorned other villagers for their lack of discipline and sloth. She now makes a resolution to approach them – as well as herself – with a loving heart.

Questions

Is there another way?
Is it all right to go slow?
Which direction would you like to move in?
How much energy do you put into 'negative' thinking?
In what way do you feel helpless and rooted to the spot?
Do you take regular 'time out' for positive contemplation?
What message could your physical ailments be giving you?

How comfortable are you with the thought that our experience is the result of what we think?

How often is an important loving response cut short by something else that 'has to be done'?

Is there someone you are scornful of who does not deserve that scorn?

What if everyone worldwide listened to what their bodies are telling them?

GLOBAL VILLAGER 59: CONTENTEDNESS

Man aged 54 from Borneo, Indonesia
Muslim, literate, speaks Malay

A man is dreaming of himself as a tiny figure who is looking into the throat of a huge, green flower. It is a rafflesia arnoldii bloom, the biggest flower in the world which can grow up to one metre wide. Despite its huge size, it has no roots and no leaves, just fine threads penetrating the tissue of a rainforest vine. A feeling of headiness engulfs him as he peers down into the flower and – in a moment of recklessness – he feels he would like to throw himself in. He feels that he is teetering on the edge of a ravine, and this is thrilling but also frightening. He wakes up from the dream shaking with excitement, but also covered in a cold sweat. He washes, dismissing dreams as irrational, and returns to bed.

But he has not succeeded in washing the memory away. The feeling that he is standing on the edge of an abyss accompanies him throughout the next day and he is strangely restless. For the first time, he realizes he is alienated from everyone around him. While the man has heard about such flowers in the forest, he has never actually seen one or had anything to do with one. Finally, the sense that he is in some sort of imminent danger is so intense that he makes enquiries and finds someone who knows where rafflesias grow. He now believes that the flower is trying to give him a message.

After several hours of walking through the forest, they find a huge rafflesia and the man approaches it very slowly, in anticipation of the strong feelings it may invoke. He is struck by the unpleasant pungent smell and its enormous size. It is very obviously a parasite, drawing all sustenance through a thin root which has latched on to another plant. He steps back in consternation, realizing that that he behaves in much the same way as the plant. He is often egoistic, provocative and demanding. His low self-esteem impels him to blow himself up out of all proportion, trying to impress his importance on others.

Now he knows that he does not need to try so hard, nor to put on such a show. As part of divine creation, he has no need to prove who he is, and he knows that he has enough of everything. The plant shows him which qualities he needs to develop – sensitivity, contentment, self-reliance and honesty. He realises that the dream was an invitation to change his behaviour before falling into darkness. As he slowly makes his way back home through the forest, he is no longer searching for the largest flower or the tallest tree. Looking for the smallest flower he can find, he finds a tiny orange bloom. As he cups it briefly in his hands, he recognises this tiny miracle and is filled with a feeling of utter content.

Questions

Which abyss are you about to fall into?
If so, what is leading you to self-destruction?
Do you take your dreams seriously and write them down?
Do you ask yourself what message dreams are giving you?

Do you ever provoke others unnecessarily to get a reaction?
Do you do something extreme to get a short-lived 'thrill'?

How could you further develop the qualities of sensitivity
and honesty?

What if losing your identity or losing your 'ego' is actually a powerful sign of progress towards creating a new experience?

What if everyone in the world realized that they were part of Divine Creation and did not need to prove who they are?

GLOBAL VILLAGER 60: AUTHENTICITY

Man aged 35 from Forest Grove, Australia
Christian, literate, overweight, speaks English

A young, angry Australian feels a familiar rush of energy in his hands. He clenches his fist and shakes it threateningly, condemning the passivity, sloth and irresponsibility of his colleagues. He is fearless, proud of his immediacy, his instant response in situations of crisis and his ability to go into action and take over responsibility. He is admired but also feared for these qualities, for they sometimes result in violent behaviour, but he feels that this is always for a good cause. While this makes him feel secretly unbalanced, he doesn't ponder for long, preferring to rush into the next opportunity for action. In his relationship with his ailing, anxious wife, he also glosses over a feeling of hollowness with a facade of bravado and protectiveness.

His wife's health worsens. Often, she is sick in the night and has to spend the mornings in bed recovering. Realizing that she is falling more and more into a depression, she seeks professional help from a therapist. Slowly, it becomes clear that she must shed her childhood role of 'weak underling'.

The man is shocked to see her rise from submission: instead of leaning on his willing arm in admiration, she criticizes him for being insensitive, dominating and hypocritical. Threatened in his role of powerful protector, he overreacts and hits her in the face. Screaming abuse, she rushes off to the doctor to leave him alone with his thoughts. He feels so stifled that he grabs a coat and goes outside, searching for some sort of peace of mind along the trails in the nearby forest. The rush of energy in his hands is so strong that he feels helpless. Clenching his fist and threatening violence as usual is no longer an option. Instead he stretches his fingers, lays his hands on the trunk of a tree and closes his eyes.

Slowly, the pain diffuses through his fingers and disappears into the bark. It is almost as if the tree is healing him, allowing him to relax, taking away the need to feel strong. The man suddenly realises that is no coincidence that he chose a 'weak' partner. Arousing strong passions in himself was a way of covering up his own fear of inadequacy. With his eyes still closed, he feels the rough bark and visualizes the tips of his fingers growing into small branches covered with new leaves. In that moment, he promises the tree that he will change. He will stretch out his fingers carefully, sensitive to everything around him. Like the tress, he will grow naturally, behave authentically and live peacefully.

Questions

Which conflicts do you purposefully create?
Do you need others to feel your own power?
Could chronic anger be a sign of subconscious aggression?
Are you limited by the belief that your opportunities are limited?
What methods do you use to distract yourself or others from unpleasant realisations or situations?
How will you change when you are completely convinced of your intrinsic power?
If every tiny burst of negative thought you send into the cosmos returns to you 100-fold, how do you choose to think?

What childhood role are you continuing to play, although it is clearly inappropriate in view of the fact that you are an independent adult?

What if everyone – including managers and politicians – faced difficult issues head on, without implementing tactics of distraction in order to safeguard personal power?

What if everyone – including all politicians, religious leaders and those in high positions – examined their behaviour regularly in order to become as authentic and transparent as possible?

GLOBAL VILLAGER 61:
LIVING IN THE PRESENT

Man aged 63 from London, Britain
Muslim, overweight, literate, speaks English

A taxi driver suddenly hears a stone landing on his vehicle, and he swerves to a halt, impeded by a group of youths who shout and knock on his window. Although he can't hear exactly what they are saying, he is sure that they are cursing him and telling him to go back to his own country. As an Iraqi who has lived in England for the last ten years, he is familiar with this situation. The taxi driver, who is usually extremely polite, talkative and ac-quiescent, grips the steering wheel fiercely and wishes, as usual, that he could go back to Iraq. But his aging mother, who still lives there, is afraid that he will be killed if he returns, and she has sworn to kill herself if he tries to visit. Instead, the family meets sporadically in Jordan. After a while, the youths depart, and the taxi driver continues on his way.

When the next customer gets into his taxi, the man is noticeably agitated, and the woman asks him what the matter is. "Home is home, Madam", he insists as he tells her about the hotel he used to own and the life he used to lead in Bagdad. Back with his family after the day's work, he does not read the newspapers about bloody riots, soaring prices and trigger-happy occupation forces in Iraq. Instead he looks at old photographs of Bagdad and is overwhelmed by memories and melancholy.

One evening, steeped in sadness, the man slumps into an arm-chair and turns on the television to distract himself, but this turns out to be more than distraction. The programme soon catches his interest, as it shows a part of the world he has never seen before – the Canary Islands. He sees pictures of Lanzarote where the barrenness of the landscape, the water scarcity, the sparse living eked out by the local inhabitants, as well as the plight of desperate Africans trying to land there in boats, convince him at last that he actually has "enough" of everything.

He suddenly feels eternally grateful that his needs are fulfilled, and he quickly accepts Britain as his new home. When young boys knock on the window of his taxi, he no longer regards them as belligerent youths showering him with racist comments, but as needy teenagers looking for a harmless bit of fun. He is grateful for the medical and educational opportunities that his host country has provided for his children, one of whom would almost certainly have died of cancer if he had stayed in Iraq. He is happy that he has enough of everything he needs. He recognises his own racism, and how it has coloured his perspectives. This inspires him to support multicultural youth projects to further mutual understanding. When clients ask him about the country of his origin he replies "Home is everywhere" or "Home is where the heart is". He ceases to linger in the past, pushing his memories of Bagdad firmly into the background, and lives exclusively in the present. He feels the fire of energy and rebirth in his hands, as if he is holding a phoenix which is rising from the ashes of Bagdad.

Questions
Where is home?
Do you feel victimised?
How often do you feel gratitude?
Supposing everywhere was home for everyone?
What good experience can you focus on right now?
What past experience do you not want to put behind you?
How often do you see strong reactions as personal insults?
Have you noticed that people who talk a lot actually talk around the essential issues in their lives?
Given that all relationships are 50/50, in what way have you agreed to be a victim?
Supposing new paths will not open to you before you decide to let them open?

GLOBAL VILLAGER 62: INTUITION

Woman aged 37 from Hamburg, Germany
Christian, smokes, beaten, literate, speaks German

A thin woman has just smoked her last cigarette of the day and is fingering the empty box nervously. She works in an office, always trying to keep everything under control, and only just managing. She plans minutely to lessen the chance of losing balance. She knows that if she does not act in this way, she feels small, unprotected and panicky, but she does not let anyone know. As a result, she puts a great deal of energy into pushing things to go her way, and she is seen as dominating. When other people take a different path to the one she proposes – even when on holiday – she is immediately frustrated and worried. Another large portion of energy goes towards not smoking more than 10 cigarettes a day. Intermittently she attempts to find solutions to her dilemma in the form of distractions, new people or new places.

When she suddenly loses her job from one day to the next, the woman falls into deep depression. She is completely unprepared for this, although she has often boasted that she is prepared for everything. During this stretch of unplanned time, she recognises that her main fear is the fear of change. The more she hopes things will stay the same, the harder she is hit by "chance".

Gradually, she is able to stretch her mind, and her perception of change as an "enemy" turns into a perception of change as a promise of new things to come. Releasing her need to plan and deciding to experiment with intuition, she sets off on an unplanned day, gets on a train, and sees what happens next: she listens to the whisper of the next river, the words of the next person, the rustle of the next tree. When she does not know where to go next, she sits on a bench, closes her eyes, connects herself to Divine Source, and receives visual images which help her to decide which path to take next. The unplanned day is so inspiring that she decides to go on a vision quest, spending a week in the Pyrenean forest by herself, in search of her own personal vision. Her greatest realisation is that all answers can be found by looking within herself.

Questions

What if you lose control?
What if you make no plans?
How resistant are you to change?
What if you release all expectations?
In what sense are you a workaholic?
Can you listen to the suggestions of others?
Would you like to be free to take a different path?
Where do you go to look for answers to your problems?
Supposing you can find all the answers by going within?
Supposing you release fixed ideas and compromise more?

Supposing that instead of getting hung up on your goal, you concentrate on the process?

What if everyone worldwide listened to their hearts and followed their intuition?

What if feminine qualities such as intuition were officially reinstated, taught and supported to further the essential wellbeing of the planet and her inhabitants?

GLOBAL VILLAGER 63: INTEGRATION

Man aged 53 from Paris, France. Muslim, literate,
overweight, smokes, speaks French

It is a misty autumn day, and a man walks alone over the bridge
which crosses the old Jewish cemetery in Paris. Although this is
his usual route to work, something feels different. He is sure he
is being followed, as if eyes are burning into his back, willing him
to turn around. In the end, he does. Directly in front of him is a
young girl with long hair and a hint of madness in her pleading
eyes. Her appearance is made all the stranger by the fact that
she is floating silently in the air, about a metre above the ground.

The man is seized with fear and moves on as fast as possible.
Though she does not seem to follow him, he is haunted by the
memory of her eyes. After work, he joins friends in the mosque
café, smoking and drinking sweet, mint tea in the small courtyard.
Here he feels enclosed and safe. The surroundings are familiar,
the company is jovial, and a large vine protects most of the courtyard walls. As he watches the wind blowing leaves off the vine,
he sees her face again, floating to the ground like a dead leaf.
Nobody else seems to notice. Making some hasty excuse, the
man rises to leave, thinking he must be ill or mad. He dismisses
the apparition as impossible and irrational – a mere figment of his
delirium. On his way home he avoids the cemetery, taking a different route through crowded streets. Suddenly he finds himself
in the middle of a demonstration that he has nothing to do with.
The feeling of dislocation and disorientation returns. If only he
could visit Mecca – his dream of many years. He is sure this
would be a turning point and a stabilizing experience in his life,
but he knows this is impossible because he cannot pay the fare.

Back home, the man is so shattered by his experience that he
reflects deeply on everything which has happened to him. His
biggest question is "why?" He concludes that there must be some

reason which he has not yet understood. Overcoming his usual habit of pushing aside and forgetting experiences which he finds unpleasant, he decides to walk through the cemetery itself, instead of keeping to the bridge, and he notices for the first time that some graves have been defiled. This prompts him to investigate the roots of violence in the Middle East. He tries to find out which demonstration he inadvertently took part in. It did after all, have something to do with himself, as it was organized by people of Arabic descent protesting against the ban on beards and bandannas in Paris. As the man continues his everyday life, he integrates everything into his world by increasing his awareness: he looks out for the small signs – the next words in a newspaper or the next song he hears - because he knows that they all have a personal message for him. He realises that the female apparition which frightened him is also part of himself - his neglected, female, intuitive side. Like an androgyne, who is both man and woman, he learns to balance the male and female aspects of his consciousness to achieve sacred integration. In this state of perfect balance, Mecca is within his reach. Everything is possible.

Questions

How do you define "madness"?

Are you violent towards yourself?

Is anyone "too old" or "too poor" to follow their dreams?

What impossible dream will you visualize and manifest next?

Do you call someone "mad" because you fear losing control?

What if nothing you overhear or encounter happens by chance?

What if "chance occurrences" essentially have something to do with yourself, pointing you in a spiritual direction?

Do you tend to see what is "possible" and then make choices within those parameters, or do you tend to decide what you want, and trust that you will be able to find a way to achieve it?

What if everyone worldwide interpreted their surroundings and fellow humans as a part of themselves?

GLOBAL VILLAGER 64: BLISS

Woman aged 52 from Switzerland. Christian, teacher,
has a degree, literate, overweight, speaks German

A small, plump woman in trousers and a baggy jumper tends her garden on the floor of a narrow valley in Switzerland. The valley is enclosed by mountains, but the woman has never actually climbed them because she is afraid of heights. Slowly, and with great concentration, she removes combs of honey from a beehive. She is known affectionately as the "Honey Lady" as she preserves a rare variety of small bee. Biology is the subject she teaches at the local school. Her life is pleasant, ordered and comfortable – perhaps too comfortable - for something seems to be lacking. Usually she ignores the niggling, irrational discontent in the back of her mind, just as she ignores her frequent abdominal pain, but today, as she passes the travel agent on her way to school, she catches a glimpse of a travel catalogue showing the lush vegetation and vivid yellow birds of Sri Lanka. She is rooted to the spot and is suddenly overcome by a wave of prickly heat which spreads rapidly throughout her body. She feels as if her world is falling apart. Turning slowly, she returns home and rings the school to say she has suddenly been taken ill.

Back home she cannot forget the amazing scenery in the travel brochure. Despite feeling ill, and despite a rising feeling of fear, she drags herself to the phone and calls up the travel agent. Within minutes, she has booked a holiday in Sri Lanka, and then she lies down to rest. Almost immediately, her fever is down, but the fever of excitement stays with her until the date of her departure. Sri Lanka turns out to be the huge, tropical garden she imagined. On an excursion to Sigyria, a huge rock, the view of the jungle is stunning. She gingerly climbs a narrow, iron ladder to the top, accompanied by a handsome Sri Lankan guide. To her left, also clinging to the rock face, are massive black beehives swarming with jungle bees. They are huge, loud and vigorous. In fact, everything she experiences on this trip appears to take on massive dimensions. She stands with arms outstretched, elated by vistas of thick, steaming jungle which spread out before her to the distant horizon.

She also stares down at the ruins of the palace where a king and his 500 wives used to live, over a thousand years ago. She suddenly realizes why she barely skims the topic of sexuality in her school classes – she has not been living life to the full in all its glory. Looking over the jungle, she can hardly make out where it meets the sky. When she returns to Switzerland, she resolves to revolutionise her lessons and climb up out of the valley once a week to remind herself that there will always be more horizons to reach for, and more blissful situations to experience.

Questions

Are you ignoring what your body wants to say to you?

How can you live your sexuality more?

Which mountain must you climb to gain a new perspective?

Is there anything lacking in your life?

What fear is actually showing you the way to go?

Are you aware that there will always be a new horizon,
and a new star to reach for?

What if everyone in the world decided to live their lives in awareness of abundance and experiencing bliss
on daily basis?

GLOBAL VILLAGER 65: TOTALITY

Man aged 57 from Crete, Greece. Greek Orthodox Christian, literate, overweight, smokes, speaks Greek

At least half of the old trees in the olive grove have been felled, but the man walking through them hardly seems to notice. His thoughts are elsewhere. In fact, his head is so full of important considerations that he is hardly aware of the rest of his body at all. He is not grounded like the trees, but fluid, floating on an elevated ethereal plane. His eyes gaze into the middle distance, worrying about the pretence he has upheld for the last couple of years. With his increased religious activities, he feels less and less physically attracted to his wife, and he tries to keep this a secret.

When he returns home, his wife asks him to accompany her to the local restaurant that evening where friends are meeting. Later, there will be dancing. The man makes some excuse and his wife loses her temper, complaining that they never do anything together any more. She insists that if they do not go on holiday somewhere together, to a place of her choice, she will leave. The man is shocked at her sudden outburst, and even more shocked at the thought of the scandal that would ensue if she leaves him. Reluctantly, he agrees, despite the pain of setting aside his religious duties.

The couple leave for Malta for a few days. During a visit to the amazing ruins of the Temple of the Great Mother, the man is struck by the fact that this holy building does have the traditional shape of the cross, but the rounded curves of a womb. In the company of his wife, and in appreciation of the feminine principle, he remembers that the cross symbolises the integration of opposites - of heaven and earth, of spirituality in a physical body – thus achieving totality. The man learns to love his wife in a new way, recognising her as a goddess, partly Divine, partly material.

Sexuality and spirituality turn into two sides of the same coin. He re-examines his sexual education (or lack of it) to see how he has come to develop these feelings that sex is something 'base', un-related to higher things.

By the time they return home from their trip, the man's feet are firmly on the ground. Dancing is a method he uses to ground himself further. Crete's traditional spiralling crane dance encourages him to reflect on the crane as a bringer of life and as a sacred symbol in many of the world's cosmologies. His love of the Divine extends to encompass the ancient olive trees, the black and white butterflies and the never-ending motion of the sea. He plants saplings with loving care, watering them every day. Never before has the man been so aware of his surroundings with this degree of totality and intensity. Everything is a miracle. Through his observations of nature, he develops absolute trust in the Divine and lives every moment as his last.

Questions

Which part of your nature is 'cut off'?
What divine miracle are you overlooking?
How long will you pretend that everything is all right?
When did you last contemplate the marvels of nature?
How can you integrate opposites so that you feel whole?
Could dancing be a good method of grounding yourself?

What fear or belief lies behind your inability to enjoy
certain aspects of your life?

What ideal or principle makes you feel superior to others
and separates you from others?

What if everyone learned to feel and express love
for all beings?

GLOBAL VILLAGER 66: HUMOUR

Man aged 25 from Lisbon, Portugal. Christian,
lives in poverty, undernourished, literate,
drinks, smokes, speaks Portuguese

A man with slouching shoulders wanders through the streets of
Lisbon. Although he is quite young, he moves slowly, without energy, with his eyes on the ground. Some distance away is a very
brightly clothed performing clown, trying to attract the attention of
passers-by.

The man doesn't notice the clown until the last minute, until he is
standing right in front of him. He is astonished to suddenly see a
pair of ridiculously large red shoes blocking his path. The clown
tweaks his nose and blows a trumpet. Other people laugh, but
the man is not in a laughing mood. He is angry because the clown
has absolutely no idea of the terrible situation he is in, and he
turns away insulted.

Again, the man is walking through the streets of Lisbon. This
time, when he sees the clown, he laughs immediately like a child,
although his personal situation is not much better than before. He
also sees that even the clown, who laughs during performances,
can be serious at times. The man realises that life is an adventure, and can change at any moment. He sits down to watch the
clown, fascinated by his flexibility, his diversity of moods, ges-
tures and voices, expressing whole palettes of emotions. The
man realizes that his own range of expression is severely limited.
The more time he spends with the clown, the more he develops
the ability to suddenly change his mood or perspectives from one
minute to the next, discovering that he can make other people
laugh, just like the clown. As a result of these experiments, he
eventually he ceases to wallow in self-pity and turns to humour
instead. As such he serves as inspiration to everyone he meets.

Questions

Can you laugh at yourself?

Do you feel sorry for yourself?

Are you happy with your role?

How could you inspire others more?

Do you make efforts to understand others?

How often do you feel that you are on stage?

How often do you feel that you are not understood?

How often is this just your imagination?

What would you do now if this day was your last?

Can you laugh on the spur of the moment,
irrespective of your situation?

Which situation, if you were not personally involved in it, and if
you could recognise its absurdity, would make you laugh?

What would happen if you encouraged absurd behaviour,
to expose its absurdity, instead of getting irate?

How would your life change if you played it like a game,
and laughed more?

Children love to laugh and giggle: how would the world change
if this ability was continued into adulthood?

GLOBAL VILLAGER 67: RECEPTIVITY

Girl aged 9 from Hebron in the West Bank. Muslim,
lives in poverty, is undernourished, literate, speaks Arabic

Cradled in the arms of her father, the young girl can feel the hard
metal edge of a rifle against her back. This is the position in which
she feels most secure. She is used to the sound of shouts, of
people running and of bombs falling. When no one is looking, she
escapes her crumbling home and runs along the potted road.
This is her world, and she has no reason to think that it may look
any different from anywhere else. She runs to what is left of a
dusty orange grove, instinctively avoiding areas of tension in the
streets. The grove ends suddenly at an enormous concrete wall,
but the girl is so used to its presence that she does not question
it. If she finds an orange, it is inevitably green and unripe, and
she hides it in a secret place, hoping that it will turn sweet.

A ceasefire has been announced. The girl is distraught because
her father no longer carries a gun. Her "normality" and thus her
feeling of security is gravely disrupted. Whereas her father used
to be an active, determined fighter, he now seems passive and
weak. When she asks what the matter is, he replies that there is
no one to fight right now, and that he does not know how to feed
the family any more.

The girl is confused and reluctant to receive this new concept into
her world. Was the enemy that everyone hated actually something good? With time, the girl realises that her "normality" was
absurdity. She realizes, for example, that huge concrete walls are
never used simply to fence off olive groves. The walls start to
crumble, revealing more orange trees on the other side. She
learns that strength and positive masculine qualities have nothing to do with fighting or holding a gun. Instead of instantly recoil-

ing, she learns to be receptive to new ideas and new people. Instead of being a large open-air prison, the West Bank turns into a flourishing cosmopolitan garden.

The girl receives education which focuses on people's similarities rather than their differences, and on love instead of hate. All firearms have been collected and pronounced obsolete in a world which now focuses on cooperation and love rather than tyranny and limitation. As astonishing as it may seem, all the people who constituted the "enemy" on previous occasions have turned out to be agents whose purpose it was to push the world further towards compassion.

Questions

Who do your view as the "enemy"?
How long do you cling to what is familiar?
How often do you immediately react by saying "No"?
What conflict or anger forms part of your "normality"?
Do you associate "masculinity" with guns or a fighting attitude?
How does your father's behaviour still influence your attitudes?

What if you stopped judging the rest of the world according to your own standards and experiences?
How much of what seems "right" or "normal" to you is based on a misconception?
How quickly can you re-orientate yourself and provide for your own needs?
What if all "enemies" and unpleasant situations are agents which propel us forward towards love and compassion?

What if everyone worldwide was receptive to the idea that no one is an enemy?
What if everyone decided to put more love into the world, rather than putting more fighting into the world?

GLOBAL VILLAGER 68: DIVERSITY

Woman aged 60 from Italy. Non-religious, literate,
overweight, smokes, drinks, speaks Italian

A rather large woman is lying in the sun in a bikini, relaxing at the
beach and treating herself to what she considers a well-earned
rest. She has not focussed on her own needs much in her life so
far, and is far too ready to succumb to the needs of others who
bend her will easily. She is an excellent cook – continuously in
demand – and thus she feels all the more entitled to eat and enjoy good food and wine, even if her obsession with ice-cream
makes her heavy, tired and dissatisfied with her appearance. She
justifies buying huge tubs of ice-cream because it is cheaper in
bulk. Although she still enjoys cooking, she actually does less
and less, almost out of habit because it is so easy to buy quick
snacks and cakes nowadays. On the very few occasions when
her cooking does not turn out as well as usual, she is deeply de-
spondent. She feels stuck, as if adventure is far from her grasp,
completely removed from her personal realm.

Feeling strangely empty as she lies on the beach, full of ice-
cream, she reaches for the newspaper. Suddenly she sees a
photograph of a young girl in Iran. She is only 16, and she is
being threatened with the death penalty for having sex. The
woman is shocked to be confronted with someone who plays
such a very different role in life from her own. One evening soon
afterwards, she is unable to defend herself against the criticisms
of a relative, and afterwards she gorges herself on food until she
is sick. She realises that she overeats at night when she feels
unloved and expendable. Her addiction is a way of tolerating her
"reality". Her tendency to conform instead of rejoicing in an abundance of creativity is responsible for the blockages in her body.

She decides to go on a creative journey in search of herself. In
western Sicily, she visits the island of Mozia where she is startled

by the different layers of civilisation: Phoenician, Carthaginian, Roman, and Greek. The archaeological museum has a rich variety of exhibits on show. The stunning mosaics impress upon the woman that she is a female mosaic of many parts, not a homogeneous identity. Most startling of all is the beautiful, Greek Statue of Mozia. Is it a charioteer, a lover, an angel, a priest, a princess, or a dancer? When the statue was discovered, it was just a white marble knee sticking out of the ground. Since then, it has been given a variety of roles. The woman decides that it is a sacred statue, and that she herself is goddess with divine creative powers. The newly acquired knowledge of her intrinsic self-worth and potential helps her to overcome her destructive eating habit. She no longer sees herself as "the excellent cook" and finds other ways of defining herself: she is a goddess of diversity.

Questions

How do you see yourself?
Are you what other people say you are?
How does this influence your opinion of yourself?
Have you fully realised that you are a god or goddess?
What tendency is in danger of turning into an obsessive habit?
What demands made by others, to which you usually comply, are slowing you down?

What behaviour do you indulge in to compensate for something you think you need?

What if losing your present identity is a powerful sign of progress towards creating new experience?

Do you nourish your feeling of adventure by enthusiastically encouraging new experience?

How would the world change if everyone expands their experience by experimenting with a diversity of roles?

GLOBAL VILLAGER 69: FLEXIBILITY

Woman aged 35 from Romania. Christian,
sexually abused, literate, speaks Romanian

The onset of a migraine forces this woman to hold her head between her hands. This always distresses her greatly, not due to the pain but because it prevents her from carrying out her plan. As soon as she can bear it, she continues working. Her structures are rigid. She says little. The children must be cared for. Handkerchiefs and underwear must be washed separately. Grapes cannot be eaten from the same plate as cake. Holidays are expensive and a waste of time. Her relationship lives within certain boundaries. She upholds many house rules. If problems occur, she rebels inwardly. At work, she never complains openly, but she resents that her hard work is not sufficiently appreciated.

When she realises that migraines are plaguing her on a daily basis, the woman cracks. Instead of pushing on relentlessly, she realises that the structures she adheres to so religiously are purely a substitute for self-worth, and that her battles to uphold them are actually a cry for love and appreciation. Stepping outside her "normal" routine, she goes on holiday, visiting the coast in a neighbouring country. Her most fascinating realisation is that a beach is not always a beach; it changes shape with every tide, and it is embellished with a rich variety of treasures – sometimes stones, sometimes shells, and sometimes just ridges of sand. She is astonished by the microcosms of life she finds in rock pools. Surrounded by pure nature and floating on the waves, she stops denying her gypsy roots and her natural exuberance.

When she returns, introducing the element of flexibility into her life becomes of prime importance; she regularly revises her life, casting out old structures if they hamper her new vitality. If problems arise, she now sees them as stepping stones to new experiences. She also realises that her lack of success at work has nothing to do with the amount of work she puts in; she has been blinded to her chances, confined by structure and habit, and has not always been honest or communicative. Now there are no absolute rules, only give and take, flowing without hesitation like water, and bending in the wind like grass. In her relationships, the only agreement is to tell the truth. She now offers fruit and cake on the same plate, blessing them and rejoicing in the positive energy they will bestow on her visitors.

Questions

What if there were no rules, only ebb and flow?
How do you make life complicated for yourself?
How could you become more flexible or communicative?
Which of your beliefs or customs are preventing your growth?
What will change when you are convinced of your own worth?
Is it time to reassess your priorities and clarify your purpose?

Is it possible that saying nothing is a sign that you do
not believe in yourself?

Could you be missing opportunities because you
underestimate your own self-worth?

How much importance do you attach to honesty in your
relationships with others?

Supposing that your beliefs are purely a construction of your
own mind, and that you can change at a moment's notice?

How will the world change if everyone regularly reassesses
the "rules" they live by?

GLOBAL VILLAGER 70: SELF CONFIDENCE

Man aged 40 from the Ukraine. Non-religious, overweight, smokes, drinks, literate, speaks Ukrainian

Swaggering slightly, a bulky lorry driver wearing a thick brown jacket walks slowly along the platform of the Munich Underground. He mutters under his breath that it was a mistake to leave his homeland for Germany. His command of the German language, which he learnt from his grandfather, is adequate for most situations, but he still has a thick accent. He has been drinking with a friend and is trying to find his way home.

Walking unsteadily towards a woman waiting for a train, he asks her the way to the main station. She is flustered by his sudden proximity and by the alcohol on his breath and points vaguely down the tracks.

When the man finds out that this is the wrong direction, he swears and tells anyone who will listen that Germans are prejudiced, that he has German blood, and that he pays his taxes like any other German national. He thinks nostalgically about the Ukraine, where he would have immediately voiced his complaints by ringing up the People's Voice Programme.

Feeling completely rejected, the man decides to travel, leaving Germany behind him for a while. He crosses the borders to Austria, Switzerland and Italy in fairly quick succession. In the course of his journey, he always asks the same simple questions, for example: where is a good place to spend the night, or where is the train station. Through this, he experiences a plethora of different reactions to himself.

After some contemplation and reflection, it becomes clear to the man that he himself created the unpleasant, antagonistic situation in the Munich underground. He comes to the realisation that it was his own decision to consider himself under attack by Germans. The reaction he receives depends partly on his own behaviour, but more on the nature of the people he meets. He also understands that if he communicates in a clear and confident manner, the answers will be clearer too.

He develops a deeper sense of self-worth, deciding to tell people where he comes from before they ask. Instead of apologising for his humble origins, he proudly announces that he is a Global Villager in a world where everyone is his neighbour.

Questions

Could you communicate more clearly?

Do you feel estranged from your surroundings?

What if life is an inner journey to a magical place?

In what sense are you over-sensitive or over-reacting?

To what extent do you need official recognition to feel accepted?

What if 'home' or 'paradise' is a state of mind rather than a place?

Are you sometimes misled by prejudice or misunderstanding?

When you wake up in the morning, do you envisage yourself as a happy, attractive person with boundless energy?

What if everyone in the world recognised that the feeling of being "under attack" is often a sign of insufficient self-worth?

GLOBAL VILLAGER 71: INCORPORATION

Boy aged 9 from Jerusalem, Israel
Jewish Orthodox, literate, speaks Yiddish

Night has fallen on the ultra-orthodox Jewish district of Mea Sharim in Jerusalem, and nearly everyone is in bed. A young boy tosses feverishly in his sleep and wakes up shuddering with fright. He immediately looks down at his hands to see if they are still there, because in his dream they were separated from his body, coloured purple, in praying position, and hovering inside an ornate box. They were almost paralysed, incapable of action. Then the boy lies down again and dreams that he is holding a golden *menorah*, a candelabra with nine candles, but to his horror, he can only see six. Overcome with fear, he feels himself drowning, his security shattered. Suddenly other hands appear, holding religious objects, but the boy cannot recognise them as such. For him they are simple objects – a key, a flower, an arrow or a bell. When the boy wakes from his second dream, his distress is so intense that he runs as fast as he can to the bed of his parents, without conducting the obligatory ritual of first washing his hands. He is so horrified when he realises his faux pas, and so overcome with the conviction that he is unholy and unclean, that his parents are unable to comfort and reassure him.

Even when the boy has become a young man, he is still haunted by this recurring dream, and he hopes to find a way of solving his dilemma. He associates sleeping with fear, and so it is not surprising that he is attracted to Tel-Aviv, known as the city which never sleeps. There, in a museum shop, he suddenly sees a print of the Hindu deity, *Mahalaxmi*, the Hindu goddess of peace and prosperity. She is holding a variety of symbols in her many arms. The man suddenly realises that these are the objects he has been seeing in his dreams for so many years. Delighted to have found some clue towards solving the mysteries of his subconscious, he throws his hands into the air, as if to wrap the goddess

in a warm embrace. Instantly, the feeling of inexplicable constriction which has accompanied him since childhood lifts, and he
feels light and optimistic. His enthusiasm for the artworks and religious customs of other countries has now been kindled, and he
starts out on a long voyage of spiritual discovery. In the course
of this, his own religion also becomes more meaningful. The daily
washing ritual is no longer a rigid restrictive rule. Instead it constantly reminds him that he is an angel – not purely a physical
being. Religion is no longer a group experience to protect a certain group, but an individual experience in which everyone develops a personal relationship with the "god" or "goddess" within.
The young man recognises the validity of many rituals worldwide,
embracing and teaching multiple methods of reaching the Divine.

Questions

In what way do you feel suffocated or unable to act?
Do you acknowledge the importance of your dreams?
Are you able to see a 'shock' as a form of spiritual impetus?
What new areas will open up when you expand your beliefs?

Is a sudden shock literally a sudden shock, or is it something
neutral which has varying degrees of effect according to the
sensitivity of the person having the experience?

Which daily ritual could you introduce to remind yourself of
your unshakeable divinity?

Given that we are all children of the Divine,
can we ever be 'unholy' or 'unclean'?

How would the world change if everyone worldwide integrated
or invited other rituals or beliefs into their belief system?

GLOBAL VILLAGER 72:
SELF DETERMINATION

Girl aged 11 from Madrid, Spain, Muslim,
literate, overweight, speaks Spanish

A young girl walks out into the schoolyard, jostled along by her angry father who shouts accusations at anyone who will listen. Cautiously, she adjusts her headscarf which is slipping slightly. The scarf is the reason why she is leaving, as the school authorities have banned it. She feels somehow faceless, as if the scarf frames a visage which is not really hers. The girl herself has no self-formed opinion. She is a closed book, a completed story. She succumbs to the absolute authority of her father and does his bidding unquestioningly.

If she is asked out by friends, she makes excuses, because she knows that she is not allowed to go out unchaperoned. Ever since babyhood, she has been an 'untroublesome' child who rarely cries. On the rare occasions where she contradicts, people turn around with surprise and say "Oh, that's not like you!". Secretly, she would like to escape to the coast. She has heard stories about the Costa da Morte, the spectacular shipwreck coast 700 kilometres away from landlocked Madrid. Actually, venturing only one kilometre from her home would be an adventure. Her heart longs to travel, but she can only gaze at the sky from her balcony, hoping for some sort of message which will bring change.

As she scours the clouds one afternoon, she sees a miracle: a huge seagull swerves awkwardly across the rooftops and lands just in front of her. She remains absolutely still. With shock, she realises that the gull's body is covered in shiny black oil. She closes her eyes and feels her heart filling with compassion. In her desire to communicate this to the gull, she slowly stretches out her hand, and the gull bends to touch it briefly. Then he is gone.

From then on, the girl collects pictures of birds, reading incessantly about their habitat, their needs and their suffering. As she grows older, her family recognise her determination to follow this passion. More and more, the girl starts to make her own decisions - what she wears, which emotions she expresses, which religion she belongs to, which direction she takes. She often confronts her family, but only by telling them her feelings. Sometimes she is still guided by them, but only when she chooses to do so. Respect is mutual. Life is an experiment, an adventure, in which she plays the main role. She travels to the Spanish coast, where she spends hours on the cliffs with the birds, her hair flowing in the wind. And later, as a global expert and protector of seabirds, she researches at the Bay of Fundy in Canada, the northern home of thousands of sandpipers who migrate 1,900 miles each year to South America. It is there that she realises that her own journey never ends.

Questions

When did you last cry?
What do you really want to do?
How often do you make excuses?
Do you express the full range of emotions?
Have you decided to relinquish any part of yourself?
Have you decided to succumb to the power of another?
What picture do others have of you, and is that really you?
What attractive but 'dangerous' experience is beckoning to you?

Do you feel you are playing a part in a play which has little to do with you, and how long do you intend to continue acting?

How do you react when you feel you have not been heard, and do you listen to others?

What will change when we all express joy, anger, love, sorrow, surprise and pain immediately when they arise?

GLOBAL VILLAGER 73: APPRECIATION

Girl aged 13 from Shebin El Kom, Egypt
Muslim, literate, speaks Arabic

A small, hunched figure is on her way to school, lowering her eyes whenever anyone passes. She flicks a piece of dirt off her blue and white uniform which she tries to keep as clean as possible. But her white blouse will always look discoloured and dingy because her family is too poor to afford soap and bleach. One of her major fears is contracting bilharzia from washing herself in the slow-moving canal, or catching the disease which killed her mother, but her face is always inscrutable under her blue head-scarf. She enters a schoolroom where other girls are dressed similarly, but no one turns to greet her because she is friendless. They learn by rote from a stern woman teacher, in fact the girl's life is populated with authoritarian figures who tell her what to do and what is so. She believes them, though an old woman once foretold that she would one day rebel and make her own decisions; like her ancestors, the ancient Egyptians, she would enter a labyrinth with a problem and come out with the answer, but the girl is so intimidated that it does not occur to her to ask any questions. She lives in fear of her brothers, her father and her impending circumcision ceremony. She has already been promised in marriage to an older man she has never seen.

Circumcision is a fearful and painful process for the girl. Afterwards, surrounded by older women who comfort her, she feels able to let go, to express the fear and sadness which has been building up inside her all her life. She is suddenly aware of supportive, unseen beings standing in a line of protection behind her; these are all women - her mother, grandmother and other maternal ancestors who support her in spirit, but of whom she has so far been unaware.

With their help, the girl gradually discovers her inner strength – a new voice previously suppressed by fear – and a sense of her own self-worth. She realises she is not alone, that other women are also daring to cross the threshold of the labyrinth, and she enjoys their solidarity. She deliberately befriends others, and finds that in her turn, she is no longer 'friendless'. With time, she develops a sense of personal power and creativity, realising that there is no need to enter any labyrinth or seek answers elsewhere because she herself is part of the divine thread. She starts to see her life and the lives of those around her in a much larger context. During a visit to the Great Pyramid in Cairo, where she spends some time quietly contemplating the huge stone trough in its interior, she experiences vibrations of exhilaration. Suddenly she hears an inner voice which confirms that her increasing ability to appreciate others is pivotal to her own happiness.

Questions

How often is your face 'inscrutable'?
What would happen if you communicated your fear?
How often do you appreciate, praise or befriend others?
How much longer do you intend to compromise yourself?
When did you last face 'authority' and make your voice heard?
If you entered a labyrinth, which vital question would you pose?

Which misunderstanding has occurred due to delaying the
expression of your emotions?
In which way have you allowed yourself to be hurt,
'circumcised' or sexually used?
Is there anyone to whom you feel 'promised'
(or to whom you feel a duty) against your will?
Are you aware of the support that is available to you in this
physical world and in the spiritual realm?
What if everyone worldwide realised that help from
other realms is available?

GLOBAL VILLAGER 74:
AWARENESS OF CYCLES

Girl aged 5 from Namibe, Angola. Christian, lives in poverty and is undernourished, has unsafe drinking water, speaks Luyana

A young child sits very still, in total isolation, at the edge of the desert. Her eyes are turned to the heavens. When someone asks what she is doing, she replies that she is watching her mother, and she does not answer any further questions. The child is convinced that if she looks long enough, she will see the thin figure of her ailing mother floating above her in a black bubble. The girl is almost unaware of her body. Hunger, a dull aching pain in her abdomen, is nothing compared to the pain in her heart as she searches in vain for her mother. The child cannot understand her inexplicable disappearance and misses her warmth and protection. She is totally isolated and rejects all kindnesses.

A couple of weeks later, the girl is told that her mother has been found dead, and at last she is able to cry. A woman takes her in her arms and whispers to her that we are all brothers and sisters, fathers and mothers, and the girl realizes that she is not alone. She sees all the other people around her. Her family is everywhere and she is connected to everyone. The girl regains her energy and starts to jump and skip with the members of her new universal family. Later on, when she is older, she discovers that she is able to communicate with her dead mother whenever she wishes. She knows that life is an eternal and ongoing story with many cycles, and that she will eventually be reunited with her mother in a dimension outside of her present experience. Whenever she feels low, she looks down at the bracelet she was given as a child, in her time of great sorrow: it takes the form of a snake which swallows its own tail and constantly recreates itself. It is both dark and light, representing the dual and cyclical nature of all things.

Questions

Which grief have you not yet expressed?
How does your preoccupation with one person
block your relationship to others and to yourself?
Do you respond automatically to or against offers of help?
How often is your mind or head so full that you ignore your body?
How would your behaviour change if everyone was your family?
Are you aware of the multitude of "spaces" and "lives" through
which you eternally travel?
What if everyone could view their lives and the lives of others
within the context of eternal cycles?

GLOBAL VILLAGER 75: EMOTIONAL DETACHMENT

Global Villager 75 as portrayed in
THE WORLD-REALITY
By Rosie Jackson

GLOBAL VILLAGER 75:
EMOTIONAL DETACHMENT

Woman aged 50 from Isiro, Democratic Republic of Congo.
Christian, literate, lives in poverty and is undernourished,
has unsafe drinking water, sexually abused, speaks Swahili

In the midst of a war-ravaged land, a woman prays in a small,
makeshift Catholic church, her eyes firmly closed. She is trying
to remain calm, but she cannot stop thinking about all those who
have died in the bloodshed. She herself feels like the Christ Jesus, nailed to the cross, with no possibility of escape. In her
mind's eye, she sees the dark profile of her own face emerging,
bodiless, with blood pouring out of her neck onto a crucifixion
scene. She tries to push this image out of her mind. To ward it
off, she pleads with the Divine to protect her 15-year old grandson who has suddenly disappeared without trace. She is convinced that he has been approached by soldiers and that he has
been forced to join the militia. And she prays for her daughter
who works as a prostitute on the trucker road between Ruanda
and the Congo. She feels completely numbed and helpless without her loved ones, and she is stricken with anxiety about their
fate. Praying is the only thing she can do.

Suddenly, she hears a familiar shout, and at that precise moment, a sharp incisive pain in her neck suddenly takes her breath
away. She opens her eyes and sees her grandson waving to her
from the distance. She has been worrying for nothing. She realises that her happiness is too closely connected with her children
and grandchildren, and that she puts an extraordinary amount of
effort into her role as a mother which leaves her feeling tired, her
personal needs unfulfilled, and the feeling that she is only half
alive. She realises that she has spent all of her life so far in the
role of servant, and that she must develop self-respect and detachment if she is not to become seriously ill.

In a dream, she is given a method of self-protection – visualising herself flooded with white light inside a pyramid - which she employs rigorously in moments of imbalance. She decides to wear a bright orange bandanna to serve as a reminder to protect her head and herself. Now that she no longer focusses entirely on others, she sees everything from a different perspective and becomes 'whole'. The pain in her neck never resurfaces, and instead of lingering in the negative energy of suffering, and in the conviction that she is helpless in the face of 'fate', she is now accompanied by the energy of "resurrection".

Questions

What if you were not controlled by 'fate'?

What would you see if you looked in a different direction?

In what way are you a servant, and do you like this position?

How does your feeling of responsibility towards others diminish your responsibility towards yourself?

How might the 'dreadful' things around you reflect the 'dreadful' things you demand of yourself?

What would change if we all went into action instead of feeling helpless?

Do you tend for pray for assistance, or can you say "I will heed the signs and do what Divine intuition shows me to do?"

Which situation might improve if you could step away from it with a sense of emotional detachment?

How would the world change if learning self-respect was an integral part of our education?

GLOBAL VILLAGER 76: PATIENCE

Boy aged 11 from Karima, Sudan. Sunni Muslim, lives in poverty and is undernourished, speaks Kenuzi-Dongola

A boy sits on a rock near the old pyramids at El Kurru. Although his hands are folded, he feels inwardly restless. The sun, a perfect tangerine orb, sinks slowly towards the horizon, but the boy gazes with sullen indifference across the desert. The beggar behind him, stumbling through the sand on one leg, fails to gain his attention. The boy is restless, with nothing to do. Sometimes he has fantastic visions of himself living in a large house with enough to eat every day. This vision drives him to offer his services to a wealthy man traveling through Karima. The man laughs, calling him an impatient ignorant boy with nothing to offer.

Desperate for food, the boy sits on the rock and cries. Again, the one-legged beggar passes him, moving forward with infinite patience and determination. The boy suddenly stops crying and watches how the beggar approaches other people, slowly and graciously, exchanging nods here and there, and offering words of wisdom for a bite of food. The boy's senses are suddenly sharpened in a way he has never felt before. Intensely aware of his surroundings, he wonders at the vastness of the desert and considers the millions of grains of sand, and he suddenly feels compassion for the one-legged man. Now he is alert to the present and curious about the past, about the people who actually lived in the pyramids so long ago. He knows intuitively that everything around him has some connection to himself, and his feeling of empathy goes beyond the usual, strong tribal bonds which have so far encouraged competition with fellow tribes.

During the day, the boy develops a certain methodical slowness and a curiosity for learning new trades and acquiring information. Building up his skills and knowledge in this gradual way, he is eventually in a position to offer his services to a wealthy family.

His patient step-by step approach enables him to realise his dream of living in a big house with adequate meals. At dusk, he takes delight in the music of a stringed instrument, played by a musician at the pyramids. Waiting for the sun to set turns into a holy evening ritual which fills him with appreciation and gratitude. The beauty of the darkening sky pours peace into his soul as he rolls down the enormous soft sand hills on his way home.

Questions

In what way are your senses 'dulled'?

Could you be more attentive to others?

What if you offered someone your help?

Can you see the world in a grain of sand?

Does your inability to set a large goal lie in the failure to see that it consists of many small steps?

Given that any dream can be achieved by a gradual step-by-step approach, what will you do next?

What would change in the world if no-one had anything to fear from others, and if no-one regarded anyone else as competition?

"Let compassion take the lead. Be patient. Do not judge. It is not that you cannot understand another person; it is that you have not dug deep enough to find that which would help you understand"

From THE COMPLETE SERAPHIN MESSAGES

GLOBAL VILLAGER 77:
LIVING FULL POTENTIAL

African woman aged 46 from Saint-Louis in Senegal. Muslim, lives in poverty and is undernourished, sexually abused, speaks Wolof

A rather hesitant, retiring Muslim woman is aware of the wrinkles of worry which line her face, but feels helpless to combat them. She wears a blue headscarf which extends to swathe her whole body so that she resembles a snake. Her hands and feet are literally and psychologically "tied". Resigned to living within certain limits, she is enveloped by a feeling of fatalism and passivity. She adheres to certain codes of polite behaviour, never really communicating how desperate she feels, but her snake-like body indicates that she has the potential to shed her skin in future and to emerge a changed being capable of plunging into action.

Trying to find some peace of mind, she walks along the lakeside where a number of pelicans are stretching their wings and splashing in the shallows, creating ripples in every direction. On a sudden impulse, she sits down to watch them. They toss huge fish into their expandable beaks and flexible throats. The woman feels as if she only has one wing, as if one side is stifled, unlived or unknown to herself.

The woman is suddenly filled with the urge to expand, widen her experiences and break her self-imposed limitations. When she gets up she is astounded to see that two hours have passed. Feeling renewed and exalted by her visit to the pelicans, she learns to show more of herself, creating ripples and stretching out her arms like the pelicans' wings. With time, her new-found spontaneity turns her life into a pure expression of joy. She learns to visualise her future, making it as abundant and attractive as possible. Like a snake which throws off its old skin, she knows that she always has the potential for transformation.

Questions

When will your golden age begin?

How have you tied up your own hands?

How long do you take to make a decision?

What fear prevents you from exposing yourself?

Which codes of behaviour would you like to break?

Which skin (or situation, or person, or ideal, or emotion)
is getting too tight for you?

What potential would explode if you gave it more attention?

If the world ended tomorrow, what would you do next?

Why don't you do it now?

Can you visualise the future you wish for,
making it as attractive as possible?

What if everyone in the whole world were capable of:
 leaving the past behind them,
learning from their experiences and
starting anew on a regular basis?

*"You will radically rearrange your thoughts, your friends,
your situations, your past experiences, your future hopes,
your intentions and your dreams into new godly categories"*

From THE COMPLETE SERAPHIN MESSAGES

GLOBAL VILLAGER 78: SINGLEMINDEDNESS

Woman aged 40 from Tunis, Tunisia. Muslim,
smokes, literate, speaks Arabic

An elegantly dressed woman is holding a pile of files in her arms.
Behind her are shelves loaded with books and papers. This is her
newspaper office in an old French colonial building in the centre
of Tunis. Her face is thin and pinched, with lines of stress and
worry marking her forehead, and she is wondering when (despite
her constant cough and respiratory problems) she will have time
to snatch her next cigarette. While she gives the impression of
being a quick, busy and efficient journalist, she is actually
plagued by indecision and fatigue. Her daughter is continually
asking for help, her colleagues require guidance, and her husband needs support and legal defence following imprisonment
for unionist activities. Torn between her work, her ideals and the
needs of her family, her inner conflict means that she is under
continuous pressure, attempting to satisfy multiple camps, forcing her to pursue an exhausting and hectic existence.

Suddenly she hears unfamiliar voices and footsteps in the hall-
way, and she drops the files in fear, immediately suspecting that
secret police have come to put her under house arrest again. But
then the voices dissipate into nothing. As the woman attempts to
pick up the files, she is suddenly overcome by a serious attack of
asthma. Realising that this is related to her acute feeling of suf-
focation in general, she decides to give herself more 'breathing
space' and more voice.

Following her new-found understanding that outward circumstances reflect her inner state, she regards censorship of her
newspaper as a reflection of self-censorship, and she becomes
increasingly aware of her own reticence. The more she attempts
to express her thoughts clearly and honestly, the more she realizes that she has not been true to herself. She no longer wavers

in her decisions – she sets priorities and keeps to them. Her newly acquired single-mindedness impels her to leave the country temporarily with her family, to a place where her voice can be better heard. She becomes extremely active and no longer feels that she is a victim of circumstance. She learns that she is all-powerful, a part of Divinity. As she finds her own voice, she serves as an inspiration to her clinging daughter who is involved in a similar search. She develops into a leader who walks her very own, unique path.

Questions

Do you make your voice heard?
Could you be more single minded?
Which major conflict within yourself remains unresolved?
How often do you change your mind?
Do you see this as positive or negative trait?
How often do you find yourself in a state of indecision?
How does this make you feel?
In what way do you feel suffocated?
To what extent are you yourself responsible?
What criteria do you use for decisions to move on?

Are you aware that the body cannot cope with prolonged stress without producing a negative response?

Is it 'good' to cling to ideals if the situation you put yourself in does not 'work' for you personally?

Suppose we are all responsible for the extreme situations we find ourselves in, both on a personal and global level?

How would the world change if everyone served as an inspiration to others?

GLOBAL VILLAGER 79: INDEPENDENCE

Boy aged 12 from Lugufu, Tanzania. Christian, refugee,
lives in poverty and is undernourished, speaks Swahili

A young boy is standing with his few belongings at a crossroad,
not sure of which way he wants to go next. His home is Burundi,
which he fled as a small child with his family, and he now lives in
Tanzania. He still remembers the old familiar places, the hills,
and the chickens they used to keep, and he loves hearing the
stories which his parents tell him about the 'old times'.

With changing conditions, it is possible to return home, but the
family is undecided and still afraid. The boy dreams of going to a
proper school 'back home'. School here in Tanzania is just a dirt
yard with a blackboard balancing on an old chair, and his parents
cannot afford to send him there. 'Home' in Tanzania has so far
consisted of a small hut made of banana branches, and the boy
wants it to feel more than a makeshift shelter.

When a part of the roof of the family hut suddenly collapses, the
boy bursts into uncontrollable tears. He knows that this is not actually a tragedy, but it touches something very painful inside him.
But as darkness falls, the hole in the roof is hardly noticeable,
and the boy turns his attention to the sound of a drum not far
away. As he looks across to the rest of the village, he sees the
rapidly moving shadows of dancing figures from a distant hut. Instead of prolonging his grief and reliving painful memories, he
decides to be led by intuition, by the clear simple light of a candle
in the darkness. Attracted by the music and joyful shouts, he is
soon dancing with the other youths, his troubles thrown to the
wind. It no longer matters that he has had nothing to eat that day.
He is confident that there will be food tomorrow. And maybe he
will follow the family dream and return to Burundi. Or maybe he
will take the road to Simunye in South Africa, where Zulus and
whites were said to live together in peace. Or maybe all roads

lead to everywhere. Or maybe travelling well and being constantly aware of freedom to choose, of independence, is more important than focussing on arriving.

Now he lives in the present, the sound of the music filling his senses and his feet dancing with the others in the light of a single candle. He knows now that he can stake out his home anywhere. As time draws on, he learns that there is no way of not getting where you want to go, because all roads lead to fruition. Now, when he stands at a crossroad, he is actually already 'there', because from another perspective, he is standing at a junction where four roads end. The only question he asks himself now is 'How quickly, directly, intensely or enjoyably do I chose to travel?'

Questions

Are you at a crossroad in your life?
Is it time to change direction?
Where do you actually want to go?
Which dream would you like to follow?
What if there is no 'wrong' or 'right' path?
What if all paths are just stages in an adventure?
In what way do you feel that you are a 'refugee'?
How can you build your own refuge?
What if there were no countries and no borders?
What if everyone belonged to the same family?
Are you enjoying the journey or focussing on your destination?

What if you knew that your soul will always reach its destination, and that it is only a case of how quickly you choose to travel?

Are you still acting in accordance with your parents' expectations?

If it is always possible to find one candle,
what stops you from dancing?

GLOBAL VILLAGER 80: SPONTANEITY

Boy aged 14 from Ngamiland, Botswana. Christian,
lives in poverty and is undernourished, has unsafe
drinking water, is stunted, speaks Yeyi

A feeling of great shame creeps over the boy who is sitting in the
dusty yard. He is sorting rubbish, together with other youths, and
his uncorrected hair-lip is in full view. Self-conscious, he turns
away from the people who greet him. He is happier working in
the mines, where he can escape curious eyes by diving for dia-
monds underwater.

But this also takes a great toll on his health. He cannot hold his
breath for as long as he used to, so he often breathes though an
old piece of plastic hose, but this is very uncomfortable. Although
conditions in the diamond mine are horrific, he continues to work
and live within these limited perimeters due to his fear of going
out into the world and exposing himself to the public eye.

His greatest conviction is that there is no chance of finding another job. On the rare occasions that he feels impelled to burst
out of this tight, rigid structure, he quickly retreats to that which is
familiar.

Following a particularly gruelling diamond diving session, which
tests the very limits of his endurance, the boy suffers sharp pains
in his abdomen and he rushes off to the nearest medical station
with a suspected burst appendix. This unexplained pain, which
then recedes, shakes the very foundations of the boy's mental
landscape. He knows that if his appendix bursts, he will die before reaching any hospital.

Deciding to avoid exploitation and pay more attention to his
health, he immediately gives up working at the mine, preferring
to search the rubbish tip full-time. After a while, people start to

recognize and accept him, and he receives their greetings with a contagious smile. His new openness and spontaneity help him to seal new friendships, especially when he gives special finds to the vagabond children also wandering about at the tip. He joins in with their simple games and laughter.

Gradually, his new cheerfulness is appreciated, allowing him to make new contacts and branch out into pleasanter areas of work. Soon he has a new job on a boat, ferrying passengers over the river. He himself is as generous as he can be, whatever his situation, because he knows that this positive energy will flow back to himself at some stage in the future.

Questions

What are you holding onto from the past which prevents you from entering the present with full enthusiasm and vigour?

What are you worried about exposing?

What if you attached less importance to outward appearances?

What if one of your roles in life is to show generosity?

What would you discover if you learnt to release fear and take the space you need, without letting others encroach upon you?

Are you aware of your breathing at this very moment?

What if everyone worldwide rejoiced when presented with an opportunity to be generous?

GLOBAL VILLAGER 81: OPEN-MINDEDNESS

Man aged 20 from Agadez, Niger. Muslim, lives in poverty
and is undernourished, has unsafe drinking water,
speaks Tamasheq

The sun burns down on a man whose face is hardly visible. His
head is swathed in a huge turban to protect his mouth and nose
from wind and sand. Underneath the turban his skin is pinched
and worn, making him look much older than his twenty years. A
salt trading nomad, he spends half his life crossing the Ténéré
Desert – the "empty land" which stretches in gigantic sand dunes
towards the next distant oasis. His greatest fear is losing his
camel which poses gracefully and arrogantly against the horizon.
Whenever the man finds the bones of a dead animal in the desert, he turns around automatically to check his own beast, and
in his dreams he turns to find his rope trailing and the camel gone,
left to tread through the dense heat alone. His fear that this dream
will come true is almost as great as failing to find water in the
holes along his usual desert route, as this means certain death.

One morning, the man wakes in the middle of the desert to find
the camel gone. He is so shaken that he instantly turns east, falling onto his knees to pray. Then he lies down to die. After a while
he hears a very quiet, gentle voice, urging him to look up. At first,
he ignores the voice as a figment of his imagination, a result of
his demented mind subjected to intense heat, but the voice per-
sists. Pulling himself up from the ground, he scours the horizon
and sees a small black dot growing steadily larger. An hour later,
the dot has transformed into a lorry loaded to breaking point with
heavy sacks. A crowd of people are sitting on top. Miraculously,
the lorry stops and all the passengers climb down to pray. The
man is astonished to see them, but they assure him that a lorry
passes this way around once a week. They urge him to join them
on their way to Libya where they can find work harvesting pota-

toes. The nomad is completely confounded. Could he be completely wrong? He thought the desert was empty, but it is not. He thought he could not exist elsewhere, but it seems that he can. Opening his mind to these new possibilities, he climbs onto the truck, filled with intense excitement. Now, his eyes scour the horizon constantly, anticipating new fantastic apparitions. His travelling companions tell him about their destination, "The jewel of the Sahara", the tranquil oasis of Ghadames. When they arrive, the man wanders in a sort of dream through the white-covered passages which protect him from the scorching heat. He catches glimpses of brilliant colour through open doorways, and he realises that his greatest fear has turned into his greatest opportunity.

Questions

Have you chosen to travel in an 'empty' land?

Is it really empty?

What actually exists already,
but which you have not yet focussed upon?

Is it possible that your view could be limited?

What would happen if you regarded your greatest fear
as your greatest opportunity?

What if the fact that you fear something actually pulls that thing
into your experience?

What must die so that you can start to journey
in a new direction?

How will the world change if everyone is aware of the
abundance of opportunity?

GLOBAL VILLAGER 82:
REASSESSING BOUNDARIES

Boy aged 2 from Yoko, Cameroon. Christian, lives in poverty and is undernourished, has unsafe drinking water, speaks Vute

A small toddler screams so loudly that he is actually purple in the face. The more he screams, the more strongly the people around him react. It seems to result in being carried around more, which is comforting, but at the same time the baby can sense the rising frustration of his carers. In the end, they need a break and leave him to scream in the care of someone else.

And so he gets passed on from person to person, and his sense of insecurity grows. His screams become more desperate, but the cycle continues. It is only when the baby decides to stop screaming that he is totally accepted and no longer has to move on. As he grows up, he subconsciously stays within this familiar, safe framework of not voicing his needs for fear of rejection.

The child grows up to understand that he has served the very important purpose of "testing" the limits of several would-be mothers. He understands that his present resignation – or failure to stand up for himself – harks back to the time of his babyhood when he learnt to be quiet in order to please. This realisation helps him deal with feelings of being insignificant, whenever they arise. He still feels fear when breaking new ground, but he knows that such fears are dictated mainly by his past. He has learnt to accept that other people have certain limits, but he has also learnt that these limits no longer need to determine his behaviour or cramp his experience. He learns to separate his experiences into two distinct camps: his automatic reaction of resignation, harking back to his past as a baby, and his newly acquired practice of reassessing boundaries, living in the present and moving forward through a new door of experience.

Questions

When did you last scream and cry like a two-year-old child?

What methods do you use to gain attention?

How quickly do you give up?

Could the root of your resignation lie in your past?

What if you acted as if failure is impossible?

What behavioural patterns which you learnt as a baby are still part of your behaviour now, although the situation is quite different because you are no longer reliant on anyone else for survival?

What if everyone worldwide was prepared to recognise behavioural patterns linked to the past which have no relevance to the present?

What if everyone was aware of their inherent worth, power and godliness?

**Never assume,
Beloveds,
that there are any limitations**

From Seraphin Message 462:
THE UNLIMITED LIFE

GLOBAL VILLAGER 83: SOLIDARITY

Boy aged 12 from Arjo, Ethiopia. Ethiopian Orthodox Christian, lives in poverty and is undernourished, has unsafe drinking water, works full-time in farming, speaks Amharic

A young boy is wandering slowly across a parched plain of sparse vegetation and thorn trees. He is dressed in blue rags and holds a stick, ready to herd his goats if necessary. Suddenly he is overwhelmed by a strange feeling of sickness and heaviness in his legs. Despite his stick, he sinks to the ground. He would like to run, but he feels lame. He would like to go to school, but his parents do not have the money to send him, so he works all day every day tending the family goats. They have a couple of cows too, grazing nearby, but they cannot afford to drink the milk themselves. They sell it instead. The family is impoverished, still devastated by the last famine caused by water shortage and swarms of locusts. The family hoards everything it can for bad times ahead. Contact between neighbouring villages is minimal, as everyone is concerned with their own immediate survival.

One morning, when the boy is rounding up his goats, he notices that one is missing. He immediately suspects that it has been stolen by one of the envious youths in the next village, and he rushes over to make his accusations, which are duly refuted. Later on, the boy visits the village again, but this time to apologise as he has recovered the lost goat elsewhere. He offers to make up for his behaviour by fetching water for his neighbour, and so a friendship starts to develop.

Later that year, drought strikes again, as it often does in this land-locked country, but it is weathered better because the boy and his neighbours come together to share the risk. Whole communities cooperate to find creative solutions to chronic problems, such as the poisonous stockpile of obsolete pesticides that they have been ignoring for years. Fermented cow's urine turns out to be a better, cheaper alternative. The villages increase their infrastructure, confident that together they can attract financial support to build a road, and this confidence attracts investors.

When the road is built, the boy sees it stretching into the distance and is proud that he was the one who first sparked off cooperation between the villages. He is filled with a surge of excitement and starts to run, although he has no idea where it will lead him. The only thing he knows in that split second when he starts to accelerate, feeling the hard, hot concrete under his bare feet, is that he is incredibly alive. He sees that everyone is going somewhere, whatever the route, and his optimism and cooperation has a contagious effect on his fellow travellers.

Questions

Do you feel lame?
How often do you take risks?
What areas of your life are in stagnation?
Where would you like to run?
If you built your own road, where would it lead?
What prevents you from starting to build?
How often do you cooperate?
Who needs your support?
What are you holding onto because you fear the future?
Is it clear that the more you give, the more you receive?

What if everyone in the world was fully confident of the success of their projects?

Suppose that human behaviour changes abruptly at a critical density (such as locusts who do not become destructive until there are more than 70 locusts per square metre)?

Suppose that optimism and cooperation are similarly 'contagious' if demonstrated by enough Global Villagers?

GLOBAL VILLAGER 84: CELEBRATION

Man aged 33 from Ouidah in Benin, Africa
Adheres to voodoo beliefs, literate, speaks Fon

A very special and rare religious celebration is taking place. A young voodoo priest is swaying slightly in a gentle trance. He is wearing purple robes which designate his religious status. Several ceremonial articles are laid out nearby, including a bottle containing sacred objects, decorated by a shell. Tucked into the folds of his robes, the man carries two wooden dolls, dressed exactly like himself. These dolls are his two dead twin brothers who must - according to his beliefs – always remain at his side.

One day, while crossing the street, he notices with horror that his belt is loose, and that one of the wooden figures has fallen onto the ground. A Catholic priest dressed completely in white, with a cross round his neck, notices his consternation and suddenly finds the missing figure lying in the dirt. He picks it up, brushes off the dust, and hands it back to the man with a smile. The man is still in shock, but the priest claps him on the shoulder and tells him not to worry. Then the priest says "Thank you God for providing me with an opportunity to help!" The young man is profoundly disturbed by the fact that the priest spoke to God as if having a personal conversation.

During the celebrations of Ecumenical Day, a day of inter-religious celebration in May, the man suddenly recognises the Catholic priest in white, dancing wildly with anyone and everyone, regardless of age, colour or creed. A friendship slowly develops between them. The man retains his own beliefs but is able to see their limitations and rise above them if necessary. He realises that his rejection of the unknown has blinkered him, separating himself from others. Now he starts to live a life of investigation, wonder, and ever-increasing perimeters. In the course of conversation, the man in his turn acts as an agent of change, reducing the Catholic priest's fear of 'strange' voodoo practices and the spirit world. The Catholic priest learns that negative energy arises if a member of one's own family, whether dead or alive, is not granted his or her rightful place. The African man learns that anyone can have conversations with their "inner God" at any time, using whatever method they prefer, and that anyone can celebrate anywhere at any time. Sometimes, they pray together, without any specific ceremony or preparation, next to a small altar which honours the twin brothers.

Questions

What are you afraid of losing?
What methods do you use to communicate?
Could they be more immediate or direct?
What piece of the past is receiving too much of your attention?

Is there anyone in your family who has been overlooked or not respectfully acknowledged?

What event could you regard less seriously or tragically if you gained a new perspective?

How often do you look beyond the perimeters of your own beliefs or convictions?

What if everyone worldwide was less rigid in their religious beliefs?

What if everyone worldwide was a believer in direct communication?

GLOBAL VILLAGER 85: GENEROSITY

Man aged 55 from Taraba, Nigeria, Africa. Christian,
rich, literate, overweight, smokes, speaks Tiv

Although the tribal chief has turned into an oil magnate and owns
a fleet of 13 cars, there are no proper roads in his village. Grown
rich through the oil business, he lives in a walled villa, separating
him from the sheet-metal hovels inhabited by his tribesmen. His
chauffeur opens the door of his car and he emerges into the heat
and dust to have his shoes polished by a young boy in rags. As
he waits, he feels the quality of the loaf of bread offered to him
by passing hawkers. Then a woman passes by, a heavy water
pitcher on her head. She is exhausted because the well is so far
away, but the tribal chief hardly notices her. The sun throbs down
on his forehead and he closes his eyes to stave off the inevitable
daily migraine. Sometimes his headaches are temporarily allevi-
ated by sleeping with women whom the police abduct and bring
to him for his pleasure, but this does little to change his feeling of
complete isolation.

One day, when he returns home from business alone, the chief
is about to enter his walled compound when a village woman
stumbles under the weight of her load. He sees the young shoe-
shining boy rush towards her to help. The tribal chief ignores
them and turns away. Suddenly he is hit by a migraine so strong
that he himself collapses into the dust. He half imagines that
someone will come to his aid, but nobody does. Everyone is
afraid of him. Pressing his head hard against the ground in an
attempt to stem the pain, he finds that he is babbling in an unknown language, expressing subconscious thoughts and hidden
needs in a way only he can feel and understand. He is overcome
by an acute feeling of loneliness and cries out for the parents that
were never there for him.

A while later, after sobbing quietly on the dusty road, he realizes with wonder that his head feels light and is free of all pain. Now he can leave the unhappy childhood memories behind him and become a real adult, taking on responsibility for himself and for the wellbeing of his tribe. Realising that he is responsible for his own loneliness, cutting himself off from all emotions and from the people who need him so desperately, he tears down the wall around his villa and uses the bricks to build new homes for his tribesmen. He adopts the boy who shines his shoes, and he realises that everyone is actually his family. His migraines disappear and he becomes part of a joyous and close-knit community.

Questions

What wall have you built?

What emotions are you blocking off?

Who needs your help at this very moment?

Are you aware of the needs of the people surrounding you?

In what way do you exploit them?

Is it clear to you that lack of generosity results from a lack of trust?

Which subconscious knowledge do you not want to admit?

To what extent have you taken on responsibility for yourself and your own needs?

What if everyone took on full responsibility for others who are less fortunate than themselves?

GLOBAL VILLAGER 86: ATTENTIVENESS

Girl aged 10 from Baton Rouge, USA. Christian,
literate, overweight, speaks Cajun French

A girl wearing a pink training suit is watching television, as she
does for six hours every day. It is the method her parents use to
calm her down, though sometimes they force her to play outside
with her brother on the local wooden jungle gym. On the surface,
she appears to be a nice, polite child. She has adorable black
curls and looks healthy enough, if a little plump. She refuses all
food except for noodles and crisps.

Sudden outbreaks of violent anger at school have alienated her
from her teachers and classmates, and so she is on medication
for Attention Deficit Disorder. She says very little because she
feels that no-one listens. She said what she wanted for Christ-
mas, but got something else instead. Nobody knows that she
feels victimised, unloved and isolated. In the end, the girl's parents send her away to camp because not even television can
calm her any more. She needs a complete change of scene. At
camp, no-one is allowed to watch television during the day. At
first, she is extremely irritated and sits outside on a bench, watching the other children play, but it is not as soft as her sofa at
home. Suddenly, she feels something else which is soft – the fur
of a puppy brushing against her legs – and when it darts away,
the girl decides to follow it.

Suddenly she finds herself in the middle of an exciting game of
tig. At the end of the day she is exhausted from so much physical
activity. In the evening, the children watch films about animals.
When the children invent their own games, the girl suggests playing a game with lots of balls, inspired by the bouncing lottery balls
she has watched so often on screen. Everyone receives her
ideas enthusiastically, and the girl listens to the suggestions of
others. Her parents are overwhelmed by the change in her and

realise the part that they played in her TV addiction. They decide to buy her a dog, and the girl devotes herself to his needs, watching attentively for any message he might be trying to give her.

Questions

What are you addicted to?

Do you have feelings which no-one else knows about?

What methods do you use to distract yourself?

What radical change of place may bring new perspectives?

Do you sometimes feel that life is passing you by?

Do you feel that life is a game of chance?

What if the intensity of your listening abilities boomeranged back to yourself, in the sense that everyone would listen to you most intently?

How would the world change if no-one took part in any mind-numbing activities, creating their own pastimes instead?

"Note that a smile or a gesture of the hand, or sincere attentive listening, will serve yourself and your fellows better than a thousand trumpets"

From THE COMPLETE SERAPHIN MESSAGES

GLOBAL VILLAGER 87: DIRECTNESS

Woman aged 29 from Houston, USA
Hindu, literate, abused, speaks English

As a second-generation immigrant from India, the attractive woman with very long hair does not always find life in the USA easy. She usually wears western clothes, but today she has donned a sari, as on all special occasions, to please her family. She struggles regularly with the ways of her parents and the ways she has adopted as an American. They are celebrating her engagement to a man of whom they approve and who – they hope – will not abuse their daughter like her previous boyfriend. Her thick, jet-black hair pours over her shoulders and down her back, and she welcomes everyone with a particularly charming smile. It is the same smile she wears at the large computer firm she works for, but while smiling seems to put others at ease, she herself feels tense and often exhausted. She prefers to write e-mails instead of approaching colleagues directly, because they tend to confide in her, relating all sorts of personal problems. This swallows much of her time and energy. During the day, she drinks coffee at regular intervals, and in the evening, she takes long, soporific baths and raids her ample stores of chocolate.

Unable to address a difference of opinion openly, the woman sends an e-mail to a colleague, although he works only a short distance away in the adjacent office. The colleague confronts her, saying that just another e-mail is not going to make any-body's day, and that this is not in keeping with her usual friendly demeanour. Why does she have to be so impersonal and abrupt?

The woman is astonished, and suddenly breaks down and cries, realizing that her face wears a mask hiding dark and as yet un-explored shadows. She has a burning desire to tear off the mask and become transparent, exposing everything she thinks and feels instead of hiding behind her stunning appearance. Her hands start to tingle, and suddenly a wave of energy courses through her body. Instead of mailing, she approaches her colleagues personally, and finds the confidence to cut the conversation short if it does not serve her purpose. Her authentic manner is appreciated and her relationships deepen. When her parents put pressure on her, she states her own wishes clearly and calmly, abandoning the role of blindly acquiescent daughter.

Questions

Are you over-polite?

What would you like to "cut short"?

Have you allowed yourself to be abused?

Which repressed feelings lie behind your smile?

How many of your decisions are determined
by the feelings of others?

Could your methods of communication be more direct?

How much of your time is "swallowed" by other people?

What do you still do - or what sort of behaviour do you still demonstrate - to please your parents?
(whether they are alive or not)

What if you invested time in yourself, instead of listening, waiting or deliberating?

What if everyone worldwide showed their feelings immediately, communicated authentically and lived their dreams at all times?

GLOBAL VILLAGER 88:
TAKING THE INITIATIVE

Girl aged 16 from Canada. Christian, literate,
smokes, drinks, speaks French

An attractive, anxious teenager with slightly hunched shoulders stands in front of the lockers in a school changing room. When she hears the loud jeers of her classmates as they enter, she automatically freezes and pretends that she is not there. Memories of the time they twisted her arm and laughed at her return with gathering force. She looks as if she is worried about being hit, so it is not surprising when one of the boys saunters over to her and jokes that she looks as if she is afraid of being hit, and he aims a playful punch.

The girl draws back in fright, convinced that they are all brutal. She has been highly suspicious of the other sex ever since her boyfriend suddenly announced – without any particular warning – that he no longer wanted anything to do with her.

Later, the girl is able to release the bitterness connected to the sudden departure of her boyfriend. She realises that his freewill choice to leave was in both their interests. In harbouring this deep hurt, she has forgotten who she really is. Now she is free to move forward in her own chosen direction – an actor in her own play rather than an onlooker and victim of circumstance.

Every time she feels suspicious of someone, she re-examines the situation because she is aware that this could easily be an automatic reaction on her part. Feeling empowered to create experiences, rather than simply to react, she now approaches her classmates before they approach her, treating them with humour and respect, and she soon has a popular following.

Questions

Do you like yourself?

What are you going to change?

How often do you expect the worst?

In what way do you feel rooted to the spot?

When do you pretend that you are not there?

When has fear led you to close down communication?

What do you feel more comfortable with: acting or reacting?

In which situations do you react as if you are on "automatic pilot"?

What would happen if you released your convictions
and compromised more?

Are you aware that you can choose to continue an "old" pattern
of behaviour, or invent a new one, as opposed to reacting "on
automatic"?

Are you expecting a set-back, a helping hand or a miracle?

If expectations form our reality,
what would happen if everyone worldwide expects the best,
and if they put effort into manifesting the best?

GLOBAL VILLAGER 89: SIMPLICITY

Man aged 55 from Michigan, USA. Christian, rich, literate,
has diabetes, overweight, smokes, speaks English

A rather stout man slowly casts his fishing rod into the lake at the
end of his property. Behind him, several bags of fertiliser are dotted around his spacious lawn. He shivers slightly and turns to
watch red and golden leaves falling into his well-kept swimming
pool. This is the answer to all his dreams – living with his wife
and children in a beautiful home. The tedium of his 40-mile com-
mute into Detroit to his steady, solid job, seems to dissipate here
as he contemplates the spectacular view.

Back inside he turns on some soothing classical music and leafs
through a hunting magazine, trying to dismiss thoughts of the
chocolate cake in the kitchen, which his diabetic condition does
not allow. Lying back in his armchair in pleasant reverie, he thinks
of his next annual trek to the west for the bear season. His new
plan is an additional holiday in Argentina during the quail hunting
season, despite his daughter's protests about animal rights.

On the way to his hunting holiday, the man is overwhelmed by
his day in transit in Buenos Aires, as he has never ventured outside the United States before. He is struck by its vibrancy and
colour, and he is astonished by the emotions and temperament
of its people. As he wanders through the lively streets, his own
life of luxurious, ordered complacency seems to pale in compar-
ison. Suddenly he finds himself in a huge bazaar where customers seem to be exchanging shabby second-hand clothes. Even
more disturbing are the city's *cartoneras*, the people who sort
rubbish up to 18 hours a day.

When he returns home, and sees all the things he doesn't really
use, he remembers the bazaar and resolves to share his wealth
more. He develops a keen sensitivity to the needs of all other

living beings. In time, he is so finely attuned to everything and everyone around him that he is almost more aware of their feelings than their physical presence. He is grateful for this extraordinary experience of clairsentience which also extends to animals and plants. Now, when he returns from work, he pulls off his tie immediately and teaches his young grandchildren how to communicate with animals. On his bedside table is a photograph of a *cartonera* pulling a cartful of rubbish by hand – a memory which teaches him constant gratitude and reminds him to live simply and share.

Questions

Do you lead a life of "ordered complacency"?
How sensitive are you to the needs of all living things?
How can you introduce more colour and vibrancy into your life?
Is your life a bustling bazaar of communication and exchange?

Have you considered inner or outward journeys as means of experiencing a widening of your perceptions?

What is necessary – apart from material "dreams" - for your greatest sense of fulfilment?

What would change if you no longer indulged in activities which you know are harmful?

How would the world change if everyone shared or gave away whatever they no longer used, or whatever they only used once a year?

What if everyone lived simple, balanced lives combining work, family time, social participation, meditation, celebration and thanksgiving?

GLOBAL VILLAGER 90: TOLERANCE

Man aged 42 from Colorado, USA. Christian,
rich, literate, speaks English

A determined man is climbing in the Himalayas, using all possible equipment and support, with scant regard for the environment, or for his own personal health. His eyes and mind are continually trained on one single goal – the quickest way to the top. On reaching the summit he triumphantly places the stars and stripes on the highest pinnacle, claiming it for his nation and his faith. He is convinced that his is the only true religion, and that if everyone adhered to it, the world would be saved.

Some years later, the man has grown older and wiser. Again, he decides to climb the same mountain. This time he is not constantly on the move in an effort to reach the summit as quickly as possible. He stops to embrace a tree on the lower slopes. Now he is a traveller, seeker and nomad rather than an achiever or crusader for his faith. He recognizes that the most important path is not the one to the top but the path of self-discovery. He climbs to feel the world reverberate within him. At the very edge of his physical limitations, he lives purely by instinct an intuition, increasingly aware of the tricks his mind has been playing on him.

When he is on one of the higher slopes, he suddenly has a vision of a place in India where all religions have their own validity and exist harmoniously side by side. Instead of pushing on relentlessly to the top he descends to look for this place. As he looks through a tourist catalogue, he chances upon a photo of Ellora where 17 Hindu temples, 12 Buddhist temples and 5 Jainistic temples are carved out of the rock. When he visits Ellora he is transformed: it is clear to him that all religions have their own validity and core truths, and that it is possible to create a harmonious environment. His own transformation heralds a new age of tolerance and the expansion of a new genre of spirituality.

Questions

How judgemental are you?

How strongly are you motivated by your ego?

Is it time to reassess or expand your beliefs?

What if the path is more significant than the destination?

What if adhering to strict beliefs or principles is equivalent to standing still?

What if "truth" is not connected to any specific culture or religion?

When will you start on the astonishing and exciting path of self-discovery?

What outer journey could you undertake to assist you on your inner journey?

How would the world change if every religious fanatic became fanatical about tolerance?

"What are your similarities? How are beggars, kings, teachers, toddlers, animals great and small, on land or in the sea, all THE SAME? They all thrive on LOVE. Who has drawn national borders, Beloveds? Who has partitioned society into different castes or classes or religions, and any amount of other small groups which exclude others? Who has placed obstacles in the path of unity? Who has erected physical and mental walls to contain you? Who has devised the concept of "friends" and "enemies"? These limitations are without a doubt constructed by YOUR-SELVES and adhered to by YOURSELVES. Only LOVE can break these walls" - From Seraphin Message 169

GLOBAL VILLAGER 91: SELF KNOWLEDGE

Man aged 41 from Alabama, USA. Christian,
literate, overweight, speaks Spanish

A man walks awkwardly along the pavement, as if he is struggling
to keep his balance. He has the strange sensation that he is top
heavy, as if carrying a pile of wooden drawers inside his head.
Similarly, his mental landscape is divided into rigid boxes, strict
categories of "right" and "wrong". Politically, financially and religiously, he is deeply conservative. He rejoices when murderers
are convicted, regretting that the state of Alabama does not make
use of the electric chair. Pacifists are not the only targets of his
righteous anger: he berates his neighbours and colleagues, and
anyone else who will listen. But they don't listen for long. He cannot understand why they don't want to see justice done and have
hooligans thrown into prison. Feeling rejected and misunder-
stood, he compensates by going to football matches where it is
easy to bond with other fanatic football fans. Together with
90,000 others, he screams encouragement to his team in the
Bryant-Denny Stadium. Whenever they score a touchdown, he
claps with jubilation, and whenever the opposing team scores, he
automatically raises his fist.

On his way home, drunk after a match, the man is so furious at
his team's defeat that he accosts and seriously injures a fan of
the opposing team. Devastated by the realisation that he himself
is a 'hooligan' who deserves to be thrown into prison, he starts to
examine his attitudes in a new light, concluding that his level of
self-knowledge is extremely low. After deep self-enquiry, he realises that the world seems to be against him because he is
against the world and against himself. This reassessment of his
behaviour turns into a pivotal experience, leading to a new state
of awareness. His judgemental mind disintegrates, and his head
feels light and almost transparent. Now, his greatest desire is to
initiate reconciliation and create harmony on all levels. Together

with 90,000 others he takes part in a mass peace meditation in the same football stadium where he used to vent his anger and frustration. The meditators meet regularly to support planet earth and all its inhabitants, flooding them with the pure white light of unconditional love.

Questions

Do you feel out of balance?

What dramatic scenes do you create?

Is this to cover up a feeling of being disconnected?

What picture of the world are you painting for yourself?

How liberal is your mental landscape?

How often do you push blame or condemn?

Are you too harsh on yourself?

Supposing you decided to work on yourself,
tracking the quality in yourself
which you hate in others?

What if everyone worldwide took concrete steps
to initiate self-recognition, harmony and peace?

GLOBAL VILLAGER 92: INTIMACY

Woman aged 40 from Port of Spain, Trinidad and Tobago
Christian, literate, abused, speaks Spanish

A sleek, armoured car with dark windows drives through tall iron gates that close automatically. A small, well-heeled woman gets out and is immediately dwarfed by a number of large, burly bodyguards. The woman's tense face relaxes slightly, for now she is safely back home in the suburbs, far away from the chaotic traffic and noise of central Port of Spain. Her position as a woman of wealth, combined with her heightened fear of crime has led her to employing these men to protect her on a 24-hour basis. Her luxurious house is surrounded by walls and cameras, and she is confident that she has done everything possible to ensure the highest level of security. If she sometimes feels a little confined due to never being alone, and if she sometimes wonders if her life could take on a different and more meaningful form, she pushes these thoughts firmly to the back of her mind in the knowledge that sacrifices have to be made if she is going to deal responsibly with her inheritance and protect her property.

One morning, as she wanders through her garden, she looks into the sky to see a huge zeppelin floating directly above her home. Instantly, she falls into shock and runs indoors, convinced that this is part of a spy network taking photographs of her property. Shaking with fear, her usual controlled smile gives way to deep sobs and she falls to the ground. The household staff have never seen her like this before and stand around helplessly. One of the guards takes the initiative and comforts her, and she allows herself to be cradled in his arms like a child. In this moment of unexpected intimacy, the woman finds relief on a level that she had never thought possible.

When she has calmed down enough to listen, the guard tells her that the zeppelin is simply advertising the next carnival. The woman begins to cry, remembering the exuberant parties of her youth. Then she screams her frustration, and then she starts to laugh uncontrollably. She now understands that her fear has grown out of all proportion, and she also realizes the absurdity of cutting herself off from her emotions and from others, separating herself from myriad experiences in the vast diversity of cultures and celebrations which are so integral to Trinidad. She steps out of the rigid framework which has so far formed her "reality", and actively searches out new areas of self-expression and activity. Her greatest insight is that real intimacy is always out of control.

Questions

What if you communicated your emotions now?
How would you live if each day were your last?
How long will you wait before taking a new path?

How have you deliberately cut yourself off from the life that surrounds you?

Which "carnival" or exuberant celebration would you like to take part in?

Do you tend to cut off unpleasant experiences, rather than enquire into their cause?

How happy are you about allowing new experiences into your life, knowing that they can cause radical change?

Is there some inner truth which you have forgotten, but which you actually recognise and have known for eternity?

How would the world change if everyone pulled down the fences of control which separate them from everyone else?

GLOBAL VILLAGER 93: PLAYFULNESS

Man aged 35 from Lima, Peru. Shamanist, lives in poverty and is undernourished, smokes, speaks Asháninka

A young man dreams that he has nearly reached the top of a ladder and is just about to fall into a black hole. This actually mirrors his experience in real life. If he continues doggedly on the course he has taken, he will fall into darkness. He feels that his strength is completely depleted and that he cannot continue fighting the deadly game of war. He belongs to the Asháninka tribe, which has been persecuted for years by a terrorist group.

After a long time living far away in the city of Lima, where he pounces on every opportunity to secure guns to fight the terrorists, he would like to return to his traditional homeland in the Amazon basin, but this is extremely dangerous.

Suddenly, the man remembers that the Amazon river is always changing course. The vegetation on the banks is periodically destroyed by flooding, but always regenerates with time. He decides to deliberately change course, choosing to think along different lines, trying different food, or walking down a backstreet in Lima which he has never noticed before. As he turns the corner, three, small, laughing children nearly rush into him, playing catch. They weave in and out of passing pedestrians, always aware, always darting unexpectedly out of the way. In the end, they always return to their home - a wooden shelter where their father sits proudly in front of a new sewing machine.

In a moment of playfulness, the man joins in with the family's game of chase, and through these new acquaintances he learns to value the spontaneity of the moment. As a result, the man decides that he wants to put more love into the world instead of sewing more seeds of violence.

Questions

What hole are you about to fall into?

What if is not actually a hole at all, but a door to a new beginning?

How can observation of nature renew your trust?

Given that it is not possible to end violence with violence, or war with war, why do you keep on fighting?

What if all conflict is caused by lack of love?

Where is "home"? What if home is where the heart is? What if everyone is at home everywhere?

What if you touch each and every heart immediately, wherever you are?

Which fixed course or idea or plan could you approach more playfully?

"You are going along familiar pathways. You may be travelling to work, doing your chores, attending regular meetings, taking the same route, wearing the same clothes, seeing the same people, following the same guru, watching the same programme, following the same pattern, saying the same things, reacting in the same way, over-reacting to the same stimuli, indulging in the same escape, blaming the same source, inviting the same disaster, ignoring the same opportunity, fabricating the same trauma, exacerbating the same dilemma, inviting the same insult, responding to the same whistle call, following the same tracks, reaching for the same destination. We would like to draw you away from DOING THE SAME"

From Seraphin Message 169:

GLOBAL VILLAGER 94:
EMBRACING OPPORTUNITY

Woman aged 40 from Salta, Argentina. Christian, lives in poverty and is undernourished, literate, speaks Spanish

A woman is facing her two hungry children who glare at her with tear-stained faces. Their clothes are shabby and their plates empty. For some time now, the woman has had very little money, and although she herself eats very little, she still cannot make ends meet. As she walks through the streets of Salta, she keeps her eyes firmly on the ground, trying to ignore the food kiosks and fruit for sale. Even worse would be meeting friends or relatives who would ask her how she is. Her family lives in a poor village in the distant red-earthed hills, and they are happy that she has found work elsewhere.

The next day, the children burst into their makeshift home with beaming faces. They are breathless from running so fast, and they bring good news: a new soup kitchen has opened a few streets away, and everyone is welcome. The woman shudders with shame. She will not degrade herself to such a level, and she forbids the astonished children to go anywhere near it. The elder child screams at her, saying that her mind is as narrow as Devil's Throat Gorge near her home village. The woman remembers her mother screaming at her in the same way, and her reaction is the same – she turns away with the conviction that she would rather do anything than give in to the authority of someone else.

Despite their mother's orders, the two young girls disappear and do not come back. The woman falls into a panic. In her mind's eye, she pictures her daughters in the narrow gorge - their angry shouts reverberating and echoing between the red and lavender rock - until her head screams with pain. Wandering through the streets, the woman scrutinises every corner and every alleyway. Leaving all pride behind, she asks everyone she meets if they have seen two hungry runaway children. The fruit seller takes pity on her, giving her some tangerines to take with her, and an old man, who is selling bamboo flutes and small guitars, offers her a simple flute for the children to play when she finds them.

The woman's automatic reaction is to brush off these offers with an impatient "no", but her grief and the urgency of the situation teaches her to change. Instead, she pauses and receives these gifts gratefully before continuing her search. Hours later, she falls exhausted onto the pavement and starts to cry quietly. In the distance, she suddenly hears samba music, and she is strangely drawn towards it. It leads her to a country musician, and behind him are long wooden tables where her children are eating bowls of soup. Overjoyed, the woman reunites with her daughters and is able to open up to this new experience. She discovers that this is not just a soup kitchen but a community centre which assists not only the poor but also the handicapped and the elderly. She is eternally grateful for the myriad opportunities it presents on all levels to give and to receive.

Questions

How much do you give?
How much help do you accept?
Do you say "no" too often?
Is there anyone you are turning your back on?
How does pride prevent you from looking after your needs?
What role does your ego play when making important decisions?
How is your behaviour dictated by experiences with "authority"?

Which automatic reaction or behaviour pattern
is blocking your way to happiness?

What would change in the world if no one
turned their back on anybody else?

GLOBAL VILLAGER 95: SERENITY

Girl aged 14 from Quito, Ecuador. Christian, lives in poverty and is undernourished, beaten, speaks Spanish

A girl walks along the streets of Quito. She is a street child who works making bricks, and who earns just enough to stave off her hunger. At the end of the day, she plays with other destitute children in the streets, kicking and throwing a ball made out of old socks. Although she enjoys the game, she breaks off repeatedly, her small pink face turning anxiously upwards towards the huge volcano just outside the city. She clearly remembers feeling the ground shake when the volcano exploded violently in 1999, and she is secretly afraid that it will happen again. Every time she sees a wisp of steam rising, or feels a tremor, she is extremely agitated and runs to hide.

One day while roaming the streets, the girl follows a woman carrying an armful of red roses. She has never seen anything so beautiful before. When the woman drops a rose by mistake she immediately picks it up, and gives it back to the woman. The woman smiles and tells her to keep it. The child is suddenly struck by the huge implications of this seemingly simple occurrence: in a blinding flash of understanding, she realises that whatever she gives, she receives. Curious to discover whether the chain will continue, she decides to give the rose to the next person she meets, who happens to be a nun running a home for destitute children. The nun is touched by her gesture and takes her in. For the first time, the girl is properly fed and cared for. She has never slept on a proper mattress before.

Later, when she is older, the girl finds work on a rose farm in a small village outside Quito. From that time onwards, the girl rejoices in beauty, in every flower and leaf which falls into her path. Her once anxious face now shines with serenity, inspiring everyone she meets. In the course of her work she comes to see that nature is not something purely destructive and threatening; she now regards the earth as an ultimately gentle being who – like all beings – deserves to be treated with respect and love.

Questions

Can you appreciate the beauty of a rose?

What are you worried about that might explode?

Which fear lies behind your inability to address this?

Can you recognise the positive signs along your path?

What has no meaning, unless you give it meaning?

What if your view of things, and not the things themselves, form your reality?

What if worrying is just a projection into the future which saps your energy and detracts from your joy?

How would the world change if no one got unnecessarily "worked up" about something, and if they understood that this is a feeling which they have created themselves?

"In the end which is not an end, everything superfluous will be pared away, and you will sail blissfully through perfectly clear waters, with complete poise and confidence in your abilities, serene and content, spreading light on your way, with constant trust in your divine compass, towards your chosen destination. May constant happiness be yours, many constant service be your ultimate goal, and MAY CONSTANT MOVEMENT THROUGH ETERNITY BRING YOU THERE"

Seraphin Message 92

GLOBAL VILLAGER 96:
ABILITY TO TAKE RISKS

Woman aged 23 from Rio de Janeiro, Brazil. Christian, lives in poverty and is undernourished, literate, speaks Portuguese

A woman stands on top of a huge, red, tower block where she and her family live in a single box-like room. She has just hung out the washing in front of her grimy window, blocking out the light. When she slides back the window pane to let in a waft of air, she hears the traffic roaring menacingly below, and televisions emitting a cacophony of screams, shots and cheering football crowds. Her sudden claustrophobia impels her to rush to the top of the skyscraper, where she now stands. It is a relief to escape and feel the wind on her face, and she spreads out her arms towards the heavens.

As she surveys the sprawling grey city before her, she suddenly becomes aware of Rio's huge stature of Christ the Redeemer in the distance. The statue's arms are outstretched too, and she retracts her arms uneasily and folds her hands devoutly, convinced of her own insignificance and mediocrity. Somehow, she is separate from the writhing activity below, and especially from the elegant villa situated next to the tower block. From here, she can see the patch of green garden surrounding it. But on the horizon is a thicker belt of green. Reeling slightly, the woman suddenly envisages the jungle on the outskirts - home to huge blossoms and exuberant growth – but she feels choked by concrete, weeds and violence. She thinks she will never be able to overcome her timidity and reticence. Escape from poverty and the crime-ridden city to the more placid, rural hinterlands seems quite impossible.

One day the woman runs up to the roof of the tower, again to escape her feeling of claustrophobia, but her path is blocked off because workers are setting up a huge television mast on top of the building. Instead, the woman runs into the streets, desperate to get away into new surroundings. As she turns a corner, she sees the villa which she recognises from looking down from the tower. A man and two children walk towards the gates. The woman's heart suddenly pounds, wanting to run up to the man and plead with him to let her work for him, to tend his garden. She summons up all her courage and approaches him, running the risk of rejection. Stuttering out her offer of help, the man responds positively and offers her work for a trial period.

As she gets to know her employer better, it becomes clear to her that money is not the sole factor leading to a full and satisfying existence. The woman becomes aware of her own creative power, calling upon Jesus and the Brazilian storm goddess Oya to assist her transformation, to eliminate her fear and to destroy the rigid structures which prevent flow in her life. Instead of folding her hands reverently when she prays, she lifts them towards the sky which gives her an exhilarating feeling of freedom. She dreams of being a flower surrounded by weeds, flourishing despite adversity, and her vision of being in the jungle is the first step to getting there. In her vision, the woman feels large and verdant, glorifying in her own fertility like the giant blooms she has been imagining.

In reality, the woman at last dares to show hidden parts of herself - to state her feelings or complaints in a firm, direct way before considering the negative effect they may have on her listeners. Her expansive and generous nature is an inspiration to all who meet her. Inspired by stories about the Yanomani tribe and their belief that nature is sacred, she also concludes that the "fate" of mankind and nature are inextricably entwined. Nature can teach her how to interact with others, and she communicates this to the rich Brazilian, inviting him to accompany her on her jungle trip. When she reaches the edge of the jungle, she steps off the concrete onto what she knows is holy ground.

Questions

Is there nowhere else to go?

What areas of your life are claustrophobic?

If a storm clears away all obstacles, which path would you take?

What experience are you denying yourself through your conviction that it is impossible?

How often do you close your eyes and visualise exactly who and where you want to be?

What will change if you express your feelings the moment they arise?

How strong is your tendency to wait or stop because you anticipate a negative reaction?

What if you prayed for guidance daily?

Do you dare to consider yourself a holy messenger of God or the Divine?

GLOBAL VILLAGER 97: LOVE

Global Villager 97 as depicted in the painting

THE WORLD-VISION

By Rosie Jackson

GLOBAL VILLAGER 97: LOVE

Woman aged 57 from Huasco, Chile. Christian,
literate, smokes, speaks Spanish

A woman is resting in a kind of stupor in her small, shambling hut in the Huasco valley, clutching her heart where she feels a strange stabbing pain. After many years of working as a farmer and uncomplainingly supporting her ailing husband, she finds that she needs more and more time to recover from the exertion of these demands. Sometimes the muscles in her legs refuse to function normally and take her no further, and in general her body is showing signs of revolting against mistreatment. She feels that she has somehow sent her energy in the wrong direction, or that she has unquestioningly bowed to authority. As a result, she is now heading for a brick wall with very little time left to change direction. She feels like exploding to release all the tension inside her, feeling that her very life is at stake. In addition to her poor physical condition, she is sure that the water has been polluted by her unfriendly neighbours. It has also dwindled so much that she suspects that they have been siphoning it off. She has night-mares that she is living in the Atacama Desert where there is so little rain that hardly anything grows.

A while later, the woman discovers that the water is being used by an open pit gold mine, developed by an international company in liaison with the government. She realises that her heart is re-belling because she has not loved herself, nor taken time to talk to her neighbours nor form loving relationships. Once she has contacted the other farmers, they group together and travel through the valley to investigate who is affected by the water problem, only to find that thousands of other small farmers are suffering. Together, they form a movement to promote love be-tween each other. They also love the earth and her resources. They marvel at earth's miraculous and beautiful manifestations in the land of Chile: the condors which fly high above the valleys, the hot water geysers which turn to ice on the cold mountainside, the dust, the glaciers and the desert winds, and the holy volcano of Licantabua.

Questions

What if "love" means not judging yourself or others?

Do you love yourself enough to say "no" to others?

Is the landscape of your mind a desert without water?

Given that it is unnatural to be the enemy of one's own body, how do you treat yourself unnaturally?

Is it clear to you that mistreatment of your own body is an indication of lack of respect generally?

If you open your eyes, which brick wall are you about to run into?

What power structure is inviting you to reassess your position?

Which borders can you cross to reach new understandings?

What physical ailment is forcing you to focus on that which is most essential?

What if you allowed yourself to explode with anger in a "safe" therapeutic environment where no one is hurt as a result?

Are you aware of the miracles of nature which surround you?

What would change in the world if there were no "enemies"?
What if all organisations worldwide had positive goals?

GLOBAL VILLAGER 98: RADIANCE

Man aged 28 from the Dominican Republic. Christian,
lives in poverty and is undernourished, speaks Spanish

Feeling hot, tired and dejected, a man sits on a dusty wooden
bench at the end of a long, hardworking day. He has taken off his
soiled white shirt – the only one he owns – thus exposing the
slender limbs and emaciated torso which are usually hidden beneath his clothes. His dark-skinned fingers, which betray his African ancestry, are rough and grubby because he has spent the
last sixteen hours collecting money and dispensing tickets to passengers on a bus. He seems to be handling money all the time,
but has very little of his own.

As he remembers the bus driver's criticisms, his feelings of de-
jection intensify. He is exhausted by his daily grind and feels un-
appreciated by both driver and passengers who rarely talk to him
or give him a passing glance. He has a horrible suspicion that
everyone is against him, even his family who receives his meagre
wages and leaves him with nothing. If he has any role in life at
all, he is convinced it is a very minor one. As he broods upon
these matters, his face turns stony and hardens into its usual
scowl, into the stiff lines of combat which protect him against the
multi-peopled day.

One morning, the man follows a sudden impulse to pick up a
scrap of leftover newspaper off the ground. It shows a photograph of a well-dressed man with a depressed look on his face.
The bus driver, who can read, tells him that it is a millionaire who
has killed himself due to money problems. The ticket collector is
astounded, and they both start to laugh. As they continue to talk,
the ticket collector realises that the driver's criticism of him was
actually a good-natured piece of advice with no harm intended.
His automatic tendency to challenge and harbour resentment dissipates. Instead of yearning for acceptance, he actively greets

his passengers and has learnt to smile, fighting against his instinct to twist everything into a debilitating mental bruise. At first his cheek muscles feel strange when he laughs, but he continues, seeing the positive effect he is having on his passengers. In the end, he spreads light wherever he goes. He is often thanked for his cheerfulness, and he shows increasing gratitude for all the wonders which come his way. A visitor from Cuba nicknames him *Guacariga*, which means "rays of the sun", but which is also the name of the tiny Caribbean humming bird which is considered holy by the Taino Indians because it pollinates the flowers and disseminates new life.

Questions

What is your mental bruise?
Could you learn to smile at everyone?
How often do you follow sudden impulses?
How many times a day do you show gratitude?
What are you misinterpreting to your own disadvantage?
What sort of energy are you personally sending out?
Are you aware that this same energy is flowing back to you?

To what degree is your mood regulated by the approval
or criticism of others?

What if depression can be solved by taking over responsibility
for oneself?

What if you introduced more light-heartedness and
experimentation into your relationships?

What strategy have you developed to protect yourself,
and what would change if you gave it up?

What if everyone worldwide decided to spread positive energy,
cheerfulness and light?

GLOBAL VILLAGER 99:
AWARENESS OF OTHERS

Man aged 59 from Rio de Janeiro, Brazil. Christian, rich,
literate, overweight, drinks, speaks Portuguese

The rich Brazilian is rarely seen outside. He has closeted himself
in his pleasant villa which he has designed for himself. The style
is minimalist, creating a sense of calm and protection, though it
is not very well kept. He refuses to have a cleaner and gardener.
It is surrounded by a rampant garden. Only a street away is a
huge tower block, the home of the woman who is Global Villager
96. Their lifestyles could not be more different, illustrating the
classic divide between rich and poor, but whereas she has
peered down with curiosity into the grounds of the villa, the man
seems to be completely unaware of his neighbours living in the
concrete monstrosity which sometimes throws its long shadow
across his lawn. Due to his fear of crime spreading from the
nearby drug-ridden slums, he has posted armed guards around
his property. Although he may be capable of it, it does not occur
to him to spread his arms, like the enormous statue of Jesus the
Christ which is visible from his house. Neither does he welcome
others into his life. On a subconscious level, his experience of
defending himself amidst domestic strife as a child provides additional fuel for his present fear of attack, strengthening his need
to protect himself.

When the man's sixtieth birthday approaches, he falls into a personal crisis. Feeling that this is something of a milestone, he wonders how to celebrate, and despite his conviction that he has little
in common with them anymore, he invites his nearest relatives
and friends who he has not contacted for a long time. It turns out
to be a curiously emotional experience during which he remembers incidents in his unpleasant childhood, but he also connects
with the vivacity of the new members of the family, the younger
children who explore every corner of the grounds with abounding

curiosity. The way they pull at the locked gates, wanting to look outside, fills him with distress. Realising that it is now or never, he unlocks them, takes the hands of the children, and walks with them slowly, taking everything in with curious eyes, the way they do, along streets he has never dared to walk before. He sees the lines of washing hanging from every room in the huge tower block, and he realises that they must live one family to a room. He is astonished at the complexity, colour and chaos of the neighbourhood which lies so close to his own quiet home.

Just before returning home, a small anxious woman suddenly rushes up to him. She is barely able to say what she wants, but he understands that she is offering him her services in his house-hold. In a moment of spontaneous generosity, he decides to try this out and he accepts. From then on, his gates are an opening to a new undiscovered world, and a place of solace for the less fortunate. The man's arms stretch out to embrace the abundance of life's experiences and opportunities. Both of these Global Villagers realise that "happiness" has less to do with the amount of money they own, and more to do with their openness and ability to welcome the new, perceiving the glory of creation on a daily basis. The rich Brazilian is aware that he consciously brings change into each day, and he considers his house and the lonely life he leads in it as something temporary which he has created. Now he knows that he can always create something new.

The man also realises that his fears are often unfounded. Protecting himself was necessary for emotional survival as a child, but it is not applicable to his present situation as an adult. Together with the Brazilian woman who lives in the adjacent tower block, he takes a trip to the jungle where they both experience and enjoy the exuberance, colour and vigour of nature.

Questions

What fuels your fear?

What do you not take seriously?

Which part of yourself are you hiding from the outside world?

How quick are you to welcome new people or experiences into your life?

How have your roots, or your family, provided a seemingly "negative" framework which now enables you to make "positive" choices?

Which person do you dislike because they represent a stone in your path, or because you have let them impinge on your freedom?

Which looming issue do you overlook on a daily basis?

Is it clear that the method you choose to reduce pain is a conscious choice and that there are alternatives?

What if pain is a lie detector pointing towards the truth?

Suppose that healing yourself is simply a matter of becoming more conscious or aware?

What if everyone worldwide develops the capacity to turn every day into a personally satisfying and magical experience for themselves and those around them?

GLOBAL VILLAGER 100: RESPECT

Global Villager 100 as depicted in the painting
THE WORLD-VISION
By Rosie Jackson

GLOBAL VILLAGER 100: RESPECT

Man aged 48 from Perth, Australia.
Christian, literate, smokes, speaks English

A man wanders down the street, muttering and swearing under his breath. He is a rather belligerent man with a tendency to interfere and provoke, rather than to let others be. A certain sense of insecurity impels him to leave his mark and make sure that others know who he is. As he walks down the road to work, he regards the down-and-outs with suspicion and dislike, immediately focusing on anyone who seems "different".

His attention is caught by a drunk, homeless Aborigine on the street corner who looks at him piercingly for a long time. The Australian feels endangered and threatens to take the man's name, but the man says he has no name or date of birth. Feeling humiliated and insulted, the Australian spits at the Aborigine, calling him a drunken liar and a "good-for-nothing" who lives off benefits and does not get down to work at a decent job.

Then the old aboriginal man smiles and tells him that outward appearances and facts are misleading. What matters is respect for all beings. The Australian is suddenly taken aback by these words because he can feel them physically: they send a streak of energy, like a tongue of fire, shooting down his spine.

This is such an astonishing experience that he wanders home in a daze. With the passing of time, and following a period of self-examination, he comes to the understanding that this feeling in his spine is a sign that something is particularly true or relevant. The words of the old Aborigine still ring in his ears. He decides to treat his family and colleagues with more respect, and he is astonished at the improvement in his relationships.

From then on, he listens carefully to everyone he meets in the knowledge that all "chance" encounters have a built-in "message" for himself. Out of respect for nature, he decides to spend his holidays at an eco-lodge in the rain forest. Here he learns about a plant which grows under nutmeg trees and which only flowers one day a year. It is easily missed or overlooked.

This reinforces his belief that it is essential be alert, to see the small signs or pointers which can create major changes or provide deep insight. While he sits in the forest, filled with wonder at this thought, he is suddenly surprised by a cloud of bats swirling above him. He is impressed by their extra-sensory perceptions, and the way they group together without collision. There is no such thing as a bat that tries to control another bat, or a bat which does not respect another bat.

Instead of feeling impelled to make his mark, the Australian covers up his tracks and leaves nature the same way he finds it. Through his contact with Aboriginal guides, he learns to wait and ask, before pushing ahead, and he learns that the old man of his original encounter was not actually staring at him threateningly, but following the aboriginal custom of looking into a person's eyes for a long time to make deep contact with a new soul.

The Australian no longer utters torrents of negative words. And if a negative thought arises, he meditates briefly and visualises a violet flame cleansing him to restore his positive energy. He is intensely aware of the fact that his choice of words – whether positive or negative – are the source of the positive and negative events which form his reality on a daily basis.

Questions

How would it feel to have no name and no date of birth?

What is preventing you from re-inventing yourself?

How often and how intensively do you look into people's eyes?

If you tend to turn away, what fear or emotion lies behind this action?

Do you fully realise the power of every positive and every negative thought?

What if you replaced all your negative thoughts with positive ones?

What if our inner serenity is never affected by outward circumstances?

What if we all realise that all conflicts are an expression of lack of love?

How would the world change if everyone heard every "message" intended for them?

"REVISE YOUR PRESENT VERSION OF NORMALITY: RECLASSIFY ALL WAR, ALL DELIBERATE MUTILATION, ALL KILLING OF LIVING BEINGS, ALL DISRESPECT FOR OTHERS, ALL DESECRATION OF NATURE, ALL DEPARTURES FROM THE COSMIC LAWS OF BALANCE AS UNNATURAL AND HARMFUL IN THE EXTREME, AND DETERMINE TO ERADICATE THEM COMPLETELY"

From Seraphin Message 122

GLOBAL VILLAGER 101: AWARENESS OF UNITY

Woman called Rosie Jackson,
lives near Munich, Germany, on Planet Earth,
belongs to all religions,
literate, speaks German, English, French,
some Chinese and a smattering of Italian

Swimming and attempting to meditate in the water have made little difference to the agitated mind of this woman. She lies naked in the sauna, trying unsuccessfully to relax. Her eyes are shut, and her hands feel strangely invisible, lying limply at her side. Despite the heat, her feet are cold.

Enviously, she is reminded of a friend who receives daily foot massages from her partner, and tears start to well up under her closed eyes as she gives in to a feeling of intense loss. Her own partner has suddenly disappeared from her life, and she is still reeling from the shock.

She is desperate to understand why, but it cannot be understood. She does not know what to do with all her "leftover" love. Mentally paralyzed, her thoughts circle endlessly around her shattered dreams with a sense of absolute disbelief.

On her way home from the sauna, the woman gets into the underground train. On the seat next to her lies a newspaper with the headlines "Victim or Hero?".

At this moment, the woman is hit by a flash of deep understanding - the knowledge that she can create her own destiny. She chooses to move out of the "victim" role, accepting that the present situation is all part of a larger divine plan which will become clear with the passage of time. Making a conscious decision to move on, she turns her attention towards loving herself and loving humanity.

In addition to being an artist and mother, she has several roles to explore – writer, composer, light worker, clairvoyant and messenger of peace. Her hands are no longer passive. When she paints, her hand is guided by an angel, and she recognizes art's potential as a vehicle for furthering spiritual evolvement and change.

Her heart is impelled to assist others on their journey, and she paints to deliver an essential message of unity. Her aim is to depict the world in a universe of infinite beauteous dimensions. She wishes to build a bridge between heaven and earth, and to contribute to a spiritual revolution.

The first layer of colour on her canvas is always yellow: this symbolises the positive power of the sun, the "silver lining" of every cloud, and the unconditional love which shines through all darkness, saturating the universe. Her creativity serves to remind others that they have unlimited creative potential.

She taps into the library of divine cosmic knowledge - available to all – to visualise her 100 Global Villagers, invent their biographies and formulate the questions which transform them. All the villagers reflect her own emotional and spiritual story. She is part of them and they are part of her.

We are all part of the UNITY TAROT
We are all one.

Questions

Is it clear to you that your greatest loss could
also be your greatest opportunity?
Could it all be part of a greater divine plan?
Could it be an indication that you have other avenues to explore
which you presently block?
Can you appreciate the progress you have made in your
development, and the progress of others?
Can you release the need to know?
What if you spent a day doing nothing but following the "signs"
which present themselves to you?
Are you a victim or a hero?
Are you a receiver or creator?
What is your message to the world?
What tracks will you leave behind you?
What if everyone went within to discover and develop their
potential for clairvoyance and intuition?
How would the world change if everyone believed that peace
results from developing feelings of unity?
How would the world change if everyone lighted a candle and
made the following affirmation daily?

Love is something I give, not something I look for
Love powers my decisions, not fear
I act from the heart, not from my mind
I create my life, instead of reacting to life
I recognise my own divinity
I heal myself
And in so doing
I heal the world

With love and gratitude to all who read this. Rosie Jackson

SPIRITUAL REVOLUTION SEMINARS

In the course of a seminar, we encounter everything which separates us (culture, customs, beliefs) and discover mutual ground - the world of feelings and emotions: how we conduct our relationships; how we deal with our fears and problems; how we express our sadness and joy.

Simultaneously, we celebrate our miraculous diversity and potential. As troubadours of a new peaceful age, it is our intent to spread the wisdom, insights and loving attitude acquired during this process. If participants SPECIFICALLY INTEND to represent 1% of the global population, then their personal work on themselves will also positively affect this 1%, working through the morphogenetic field.

The vision of the Spiritual Revolution Project is that these seminars and processes take place worldwide and that participants from many countries built up partnerships with each other. Participants are also invited to search for their chosen "global villager" in real life, and to record their experiences in articles / film / photographs as part of the project 100 SEEK 100.

SPIRITUAL REVOLUTION SEMINARS: CONTENT

Lecture: HOW CAN WE CREATE PARADISE ON EARTH?

Exploring the painting THE WORLD-REALITY to sharpen perception and to work on personal issues

Exploring the painting THE WORLD-VISION to develop visions for ourselves and for our world

Identifying with one global villager from the UNITY TAROT, encountering new structures and opportunities

Laying out the WORLD CARPET (11 x 7 metres)
to gain new global perspectives and to take part in
GLOBAL FAMILY CONSTELLATION processes

Music and movement sessions to develop self-expression
and aid release

Visualisation exercises to develop new goals and gain
increased insight

Guided meditation sessions through videos which illustrate
important Seraphin Messages

Instructions on connecting with the Divine and discovering your
life's purpose

Group rituals to improve communication and enhance oneness

WHAT SPIRITUAL REVOLUTION SEMINARS ACTIVATE

- Hidden potential and unsuppressed enthusiasm for life
- Deeper, wider perception and new perspectives
- Recognition of old stumbling blocks preventing vocation/vision
- Openness for greeting everything "foreign"
- Active participation in the role of divine messenger
- Courage to critically question what happens behind the scenes
- Loving concern for ourselves, our fellow travellers, our earth
- Affinity with all nations through emotions common to all
- Creativity as a method of expression and gaining fulfilment
- The concept of life as a self-determined adventure and journey
- The discovery of new cultural and spiritual vistas

ABOUT THE AUTHOR

ART - MUSIC - SERAPHIN MESSAGES - SEMINARS

Rosie Jackson is an author, artist, composer and the founder of *The Spiritual Revolution Project*. This encompasses paintings, music, videos, books and seminars to develop self-awareness. Teaching spiritual principles to promote consciousness, her music and art are powerful catalysts of spiritual uplift. Her *Unity Tarot* illustrates the transformation of 100 global villagers in 2 large paintings and 100 written biographies.

Since 2010, Rosie Jackson has been receiving telepathic messages and visions from the angel, Seraphin. These communications urge us to protect our earth and show us how paradise on earth can be achieved. Many messages are presently available in English, German, Italian, Spanish, Dutch and Korean.

Born in England, Rosie Jackson studied German and French and qualified as a teacher. She has worked as an educator in China, and as a translator, designer and editor for publishing houses and companies in Europe. She now works freelance as an artist, author and spiritual teacher in Germany and Italy. rosie@rosiejackson.de.

OTHER PUBLICATIONS BY ROSIE JACKSON

The Complete Seraphin Messages: Volume 1
ISBN 978-3-751976-72-5 (Seraphin Series: Book 4)
The Complete Seraphin Messages: Volume 2
ISBN 978-3-75198150-7 (Seraphin Series: Book 5)
The Complete Seraphin Messages: Volume 3
ISBN 978-3-75190001-0 (Seraphin Series: Book 6)
The Complete Seraphin Messages: Volume 4
ISBN 978-3-752643275 (Seraphin Series: Book 7)
The Complete Seraphin Messages: Volume 5
ISBN 978-3-75344474-1 (Seraphin Series: Book 8)
Seraphin's Spirituality School
ISBN 978-3-749485-84-0 (Seraphin Series: Book 1)
The World will become Peaceful, Beautiful and Abundant
ISBN 978-3-751920-66-7 (Seraphin Series: Book 2)
The Peace Parables
ISBN 978-3-750441-51-4 (Seraphin Series: Book 3)
The Absolutely Amazing Activity Book
of Snakes, Stars and Snowballs
ISBN 978-3-8370-0238-6

PERSONAL WEBSITE: www.rosiejackson.de

INSTAGRAM: https://www.instagram.com/rjspirit100/

ART FOR SALE: www.singulart.com/de/künstler/rosie-jackson-32447

PRINTS FOR SALE: www.artflakes.com/de/shop/rosie-jackson

MUSIC ALBUM:
https://rjspirit100.bandcamp.com/album/songs-for-the-era-of-light-and-life

SEMINARS: http://www.rosie-jackson.de/revolution/Seminar_Termine.html

THE SPIRITUAL REVOLUTION PROJECT:
http://www.rosie-jackson.de/revolution/Projekt_und_Vision.html

YOUTUBE VIDEOS: https://www.youtube.com/user/RJSpirit100

Rosie Jackson

AN ANGEL SPEAKS
SERAPHIN'S SPIRITUALITY SCHOOL
YOUR DIVINE ROLE:
CREATING AN ERA OF PEACE

ISBN 978-3-749485-84-0. 2019. 292 pages

Seraphin is an angel who send us messages of hope and inspiration, as well as practical advice. Our world requires a drastic makeover, and this will be fueled by a universal change of heart, by widening our perspectives, and by reconnecting to the divine core within us, which impels us to develop our skills in service to humanity.

Seraphin's statements provide remarkable insights, provoke intense reflection, and challenge our limited viewpoint. With great clarity, he points out the necessity for radical change, while knowing that we have the power to implement it. The messages in this book were received telepathically by Rosie Jackson.

This collection of 111 Seraphin Messages has 5 purposes. The first chapter, "Messages from the other side" encouraging readers to start a writing journey, contacting their unseen guides and "downloading" information relevant to their particular task on earth. As your spiritual abilities progress, you will increase in confidence, and you will become a source of inspiration for others.

Secondly, the chapters entitled "Your divine purpose", "Transcending your past", "Creating your future", and "Your relationships", intend to help readers along the spiritual path, assisting them to develop potential, achieve excellency, and use these skills and knowledge for the benefit of all.

Chapter 3, "Preparing for transition", provides advice on how to deal with the intense times ahead. Due to our present position in the photon belt, our planet is showered with highly powered cosmic energies. These create enormous change, supporting everything of divine nature, and exposing that which is not. Fourthly, the chapters on rebuilding our world offer instructions on how to address practical problems. They also highlight which qualities we should manifest in order to maintain peace, beauty and abundance on our world. Fifthly, the goal of the very last chapter, "Reconnecting to the universe", aims to increase our awareness of our galactic neighbours who lovingly observe us. After millennia of "disconnection", we will finally resume our membership of the cosmic family.

Rosie Jackson

THE ABSOLUTELY AMAZING ACTIVITY BOOK
OF SNAKES, STARS AND SNOWBALLS
FURTHERING CREATIVE EXPRESSION
IN CHILDREN FROM THE AGE OF 7 UP

ISBN: 978-3-8370-0238-6

Each of these 80 pages presents a story, idea, or situation which stimulates children's imagination through questions, suggestions or invitations to wonder what happens next. The pictures they then draw are subconscious images of their inner world, feelings and desires, thus providing their carers with a valuable window to their soul.

Once children are accustomed to expressing their own emotions and needs, they are better able to assess themselves and others on the path towards mutual understanding and peace.

Like SNAKES they can shed their old skins, like SNOWBALLS they can move on and grow, reaching more and more towards the stars.

Rosie Jackson

THE WORLD WILL BECOME PEACEFUL, BEAUTIFUL AND ABUNDANT
A compact instruction manual:
150 ways to improve our world

ISBN 9783751920667.196 pages

Our desecrated, ravaged earth requires massive overhaul. WHAT CAN WE DO? This instruction book for individuals and groups presents 150 methods of making the world peaceful, beautiful and abundant. They focus on personal, social, cultural, environmental and global RESPON-SIBILITIES. Most important, however, is the recognition of our divine responsibilities:

"We are the drop of water in a polluted ocean. We are a genetically manipulated seed planted in a field which has been doused with artificial fertiliser. We are a small tender plant strangled by rampant weeds. We are a million stars in a far-flung galaxy. If we can take on these roles, we will ask WHY and search for solutions. If we are in polluted water, we will seek METHODS OF PURIFICATION. If we are a genetically manipulated seed, we will seek METHODS TO REVERSE ADVERSE PROGRAMING. If we are planted in contaminated soil, we will seek METHODS TO REGENERATE NATURALLY. If we are strangled by weeds, we will seek METHODS OF CLEARING THE MENTAL JUNGLE. And if we are a million stars, we will be encouraged to LIVE OUR INFINITE POTENTIAL AND SPREAD LIGHT ETERNALLY".

These poetic as well as practical pearls of wisdom have been provided by the angel Seraphin, and have been received telepathically between 2009 and 2020 by the author and artist, Rosie Jackson.

Rosie Jackson

THE PEACE PARABLES:
HOW THE FOOL BECAME GOD,
AND OTHER STORIES

ISBN 9783750441514, 140 pages

What do the stories with the titles INSIDE THE MARBLE and THE ROOF and THE EMERGENCY BRAKE have in common? Like the other 53 stories in this volume, they are "peace parables" because they urge us to improve our behaviour, not only for our own benefit, but for the common good, enabling us to co-create a peaceful world. Most of these parables are descriptions of visions received during meditation by the author and artist, Rosie Jackson. Some are adaptations of messages received telepathically from the angel, Seraphin.

One of the most famous storytellers is the soul we call Jesus. Parables are an excellent way of teaching, as they entertain and educate people of various paths simultaneously, without raising an accusing finger. No one is addressed personally. It is up to readers to draw their own conclusions. All these parables are designed to assist readers on their spiritual journey, opening up new vistas, opportunities and directions. The stories provide insights, shake up superstitions, encourage heroic acts, expose corruption, pinpoint our enslaved mentalities, reveal our debilitating dependence, revive our dormant creative powers, invite reassessment of the "status quo", reveal downward spirals, discourage materialism, inspire love of nature and foster true values.

The stories entertain and educate, urging us to search for better solutions, to increase compassion and recognise our interconnection. They illuminate dangerous domino effects, and expose our narrow-mindedness and blind allegiance. These stories prepare us to be flexible in the face of great change, and force us to reflect upon our LIFE'S PURPOSE.

FOR YOUR NOTES

FOR YOUR NOTES

FOR YOUR NOTES